# 1000

# PATTERNS

C22179

# Contents

# **Pattern***finder*

The patterns in the pattern finder are categorised by motif and subject matter, as well as being fully cross-referenced with alternative names and terms. There are six categories in the pattern finder: regions/ethnic origin; basic shapes; natural shapes; mythological, religious and symbolic patterns; artefacts; and named periods/art movements. All the numbering in the pattern finder refers to the pattern numbers only, and not to page numbers.

## REGIONS/ETHNIC ORIGIN

**CASPIAN REGION** 233, 234, 235, 236, 237, 238, 239, 240, 241, 242, 243, 244, 245, 246, 247, 248, 249, 250, 251, 252, 253, 254, 255, 256, 257, 258, 259, 260, 261, 262, 263, 264, 265, 266, 267, 268, 269, 270, 271, 272, 273, 274, 275, 276, 277, 278, 279, 280, 281, 282

**CELTIC** 446, 447, 448, 449, 450, 451, 452, 453, 454, 455, 456, 457, 458, 459, 460, 461, 462, 463, 464, 899

**CHINA** 54, 55, 56, 57, 58, 59, 60, 61, 62, 63, 64, 65, 66, 67, 68, 69, 70, 71, 72, 73, 74, 75, 76, 77, 78, 79, 80, 81, 82, 83, 84, 85

**CLASSICAL WORLD** 283, 284, 285, 286, 287, 288, 289, 290, 291, 292, 293, 294, 295, 296, 297, 298, 299, 300, 301, 302, 303, 304, 305, 306, 307, 308, 309, 310, 311, 312, 313, 314, 315, 316, 317, 318, 319, 320, 321, 322, 323, 324, 325

**COLONIAL NORTH AMERICA** 433, 434, 435, 436, 437, 438, 439, 440, 441, 442, 443, 444, 445

**INDIA & PAKISTAN** 143, 144, 145, 146, 147, 148, 149, 150, 151, 152, 153, 154, 155, 156, 157, 158, 159, 160, 161, 162, 163, 164, 165, 166, 167, 168, 169, 170, 171, 172, 173, 174, 175, 176, 177, 178, 179, 180, 181, 182, 183, 184, 185, 186, 187, 188, 189, 190, 191, 192, 193

**INDONESIA** 24, 25, 26, 27, 28, 29, 30, 31, 32, 33, 34, 35, 36, 37, 38, 39, 40, 41, 42, 43, 44, 45, 46, 47, 48, 49, 50, 51, 52, 53

**JAPAN** 86, 87, 88, 89, 90, 91, 92, 93, 94, 95, 96, 97, 98, 99, 100, 101, 102, 103, 104, 105, 106, 107, 108, 109, 110, 111, 112, 113, 114, 115, 116, 117, 118, 119, 120, 121, 122, 123, 124, 125, 126, 127, 128, 129, 130, 131, 132, 133, 134, 135, 136, 137, 138, 139, 140, 141, 142

**PERSIA** 194, 195, 196, 197, 198, 199, 200, 201, 202, 203, 204, 205, 206, 207, 208, 209, 210, 211, 212, 213, 214, 215, 216, 217, 218, 219, 220, 221, 222, 223, 224, 225, 226, 227, 228, 229, 230, 231, 232

**POLYNESIA** 1, 2, 3, 4, 5, 6, 7, 8, 9, 10, 11, 12, 13, 14, 15, 16, 17, 18, 19, 20, 21, 22, 23

**PRE-COLUMBIAN AMERICA** 377, 378, 379, 380, 381, 382, 383, 384, 385, 386, 387, 388, 389, 390, 391, 392, 393, 394, 395, 396, 397, 398, 399, 400, 401, 402, 403, 404, 405, 406, 407, 408, 409, 410, 411, 412, 413, 414, 415, 416, 417, 418, 419, 420, 421, 422, 423, 424, 425, 426, 427, 428, 429, 430, 431, 432

**SUB-SAHARAN & NORTH AFRICA** 326, 327, 328, 329, 330, 331, 332, 333, 334, 335, 336, 337, 338, 339, 340, 341, 342, 343, 344, 345, 346, 347, 348, 349, 350, 351, 352, 353, 354, 355, 356, 357, 358, 359, 360, 361, 362, 363, 364, 365, 366, 367, 368, 369, 370, 371, 372, 373, 374, 375, 376

# BASIC AND GEOMETRIC SHAPES

**ABSTRACT**  819, 840, 846, 847, 851, 856, 867, 875, 890, 894, 902, 904, 914, 915, 931, 932, 936, 938, 942, 958, 959, 967, 968, 970, 972, 973, 975, 976, 982, 990, 994, 997, 998, 999, 1000

**ACANTHUS**  465, 466, 483, 484, 485, 486, 487, 488, 514, 515, 639

**ADLER/EAGLE MOTIF**  257, 259

**ARABESQUE**  229, 521, 522, 523

**ARROW/CHEVRON**  18, 19, 50, 150, 156, 199, 202, 203, 252, 257, 259, 283, 344, 351, 353, 358, 363, 382, 397, 415, 752, 806, 808, 813, 842, 861, 877

**BASKETWEAVE/LATTICE**  86, 116, 135, 137, 141, 342, 343, 344, 345, 494, 597, 669, 797, 864, 985

**'BEAUTIFUL GARDEN' DESIGN** *see MINA-KHANI*

**BOTEH/BUTA/PAISLEY/TEARDROP**  21, 146, 158, 164, 165, 166, 167, 168, 169, 170, 171, 185, 272, 273, 497, 500, 503, 777, 828, 876, 889, 905, 909, 910, 913, 917, 923, 935, 946, 948, 950, 954, 960, 971, 972, 984

**BUTA** *see BOTEH*

**CELTIC KNOT** *see EVERLASTING KNOT*

**CHECKERBOARD**  1, 3, 9, 20, 101, 182, 256, 333, 362, 363, 415, 462, 481, 573, 744, 794, 860; *see also* **SQUARE**

**CHEVRON** *see ARROW*

**CIRCLE/SPOT**  9, 34, 39, 58, 68, 73, 88, 103, 104, 108, 117, 124, 126, 137, 143, 149, 150, 155, 160, 161, 162, 164, 169, 173, 178, 180, 181, 182, 189, 190, 221, 228, 238, 247, 250, 254, 255, 260, 261, 262, 263, 264, 265, 281, 283, 284, 285, 287, 289, 290, 291, 293, 294, 302, 304, 305, 307, 308, 311, 312, 313, 314, 315, 316, 317, 318, 319, 322, 323, 325, 327, 359, 363, 366, 367, 368, 371, 372, 373, 374, 375, 377, 396, 399, 400, 401, 402, 433, 435, 440, 443, 445, 446, 450, 451, 452, 453, 456, 457, 459, 460, 461, 463, 466, 468, 469, 470, 471, 472, 473, 474, 476, 477, 478, 482, 487, 493, 496, 499, 505, 506, 507, 508, 510, 511, 515, 519, 520, 523, 526, 527, 530, 531, 532, 533, 534, 535, 536, 537, 538, 547, 554, 557, 558, 559, 569, 574, 579, 582, 583, 584, 585, 586, 596, 600, 602, 603, 612, 616, 618, 624, 627, 635, 642, 644, 646, 647, 650, 652, 656, 658, 661, 664, 665, 666, 668, 672, 673, 673, 674, 683, 685, 688, 689, 690, 691, 696, 699, 705, 710, 711, 712, 713, 718, 724, 727, 728, 729, 731, 732, 736, 739, 741, 742, 743, 746, 747, 748, 750, 752, 753, 754, 755, 756, 760, 761, 763, 764, 765, 767, 770, 771, 772, 773, 774, 776, 777, 778, 782, 784, 785, 786, 789, 791, 793, 794, 795, 796, 797, 798, 799, 801, 802, 809, 812, 814, 815, 818, 819, 820, 825, 826, 829, 830, 838, 842, 845, 851, 862,

867, 870, 873, 875, 878, 881, 882, 890, 892, 896, 899, 901, 903, 906, 908, 909, 910, 912, 919, 920, 921, 922, 924, 925, 930, 940, 941, 942, 947, 949, 953, 962, 963, 964, 967, 971, 977, 994, 996, 997, 998, 999; *see also* **FLOWER**; **ROSETTE**

**CRESCENT/SICKLE**  99, 260, 714, 815

**CROSS/X**  43, 129, 132, 147, 148, 170, 203, 249, 277, 278, 280, 286, 318, 320, 324, 325, 327, 340, 344, 360, 366, 381, 382, 384, 386, 388, 389, 390, 392, 393, 404, 418, 427, 443, 446, 448, 476, 478, 479, 505, 506, 598, 752, 763, 803, 839, 840, 861, 895

**DIAMOND**  13, 17, 41, 42, 43, 45, 48, 62, 85, 92, 96, 100, 101, 106, 115, 126, 129, 148, 150, 152, 154, 156, 174, 182, 183, 184, 190, 219, 223, 234, 237, 240, 243, 244, 245, 248, 249, 252, 258, 262, 265, 268, 269, 270, 274, 277, 278, 279, 282, 283, 285, 286, 293, 323, 324, 325, 346, 348, 353, 354, 355, 356, 360, 362, 368, 369, 371, 375, 381, 386, 388, 389, 392, 394, 395, 408, 415, 416, 417, 418, 419, 420, 421, 422, 423, 435, 437, 438, 445, 469, 470, 476, 481, 486, 487, 494, 505, 506, 509, 510, 526, 531, 538, 539, 540, 541, 542, 551, 569, 570, 579, 580, 598, 605, 709, 775, 783, 813, 897, 899, 911, 947, 987

**EAGLE MOTIF** *see* **ADLER**

**EGG-AND-TONGUE**  294, 544

**EVERLASTING/CELTIC/MAGIC KNOT**  56, 446, 448, 449, 450, 451, 452, 453, 454, 457, 458, 460, 461, 462, 463, 464, 468, 477, 480, 485, 505, 506, 507, 508, 509, 510, 511, 512, 513, 551

**FAN**  10, 97, 216, 291, 297, 301, 515, 521, 600, 668, 748, 798

**FIGURE OF EIGHT**  22, 418, 493

**FLEUR-DE-LIS**  246, 482, 509, 510, 511

**GOOD LUCK SYMBOL** *see* **SWASTIKA**

**GREEK KEY**  246, 253, 283, 298

**GRID**  1, 2, 3, 4, 5, 6, 7, 12, 13, 14, 17, 21, 22, 39, 105, 148, 183, 184, 219, 223, 230, 240, 253, 314, 315, 316, 317, 318, 319, 323, 357, 359, 520, 541, 542, 682, 708, 723, 732, 760, 785, 786, 802, 847, 881, 882, 980

**GUL/LOZENGE**  154, 223, 225, 251, 254, 270, 274, 276, 277, 278, 279, 415, 422, 499

**HARSHANG**  252, 253

**HEART SHAPE**  122, 144, 216, 316, 324, 440, 443, 444, 446, 501, 511, 513, 584, 604, 608, 612, 653, 676, 678, 687, 692, 703, 707, 744, 768, 818, 822, 857, 905, 971

## BASIC SHAPES *(continued)*

*HERATI* 207, 236, 251

**HEXAGON** 129, 182, 195, 198, 199, 200, 201, 202, 203, 204, 221, 234, 259, 269, 280, 338, 436, 509, 574, 657

*KHANCH* 194

**LATTICE** *see* **BASKETWEAVE**

**LOZENGE** *see* **GUL**

**MAGIC KNOT** *see* **EVERLASTING KNOT**

*MINA-KHANI/* **'BEAUTIFUL GARDEN' DESIGN** 183, 184, 186, 187, 188

**OCTAGON** 148, 154, 227, 229, 230, 251, 253, 258, 276, 434, 724

**PAISLEY** *see* **BOTEH**

*PARANG RUSAK/* **DAGGER** 46

**PENTAGON** 762, 764

**POTHOOK** 243, 247

**ROSETTE** 68, 102, 109, 116, 117, 125, 138, 143, 148, 163, 181, 184, 189, 219, 220, 227, 228, 229, 230, 232, 284, 287, 289, 290, 291, 306, 310, 374, 414, 433, 443, 474, 496, 536, 550, 586, 598, 600, 603, 624, 628, 632, 658, 664, 711, 743, 755, 905, 913; *see also* **CIRCLE; FLOWER**

**SCROLL** 91, 120, 125, 226, 234, 246, 256, 262, 263, 283, 295, 297, 308, 310, 313, 315, 316, 317, 319, 324, 406, 446, 456, 457, 459, 491, 514, 515, 516, 521, 522, 523, 536, 537, 546, 548, 550, 554, 557, 558, 559, 561, 563, 673, 946; *see also* **SPIRAL; WAVE**

**SICKLE** *see* **CRESCENT**

**SPIRAL** 22, 52, 81, 161, 284, 286, 363, 441, 456, 457, 459, 485, 547, 582, 710, 720, 728, 751, 753, 782, 846, 855, 875, 876; *see also* **SCROLL; WAVE**

**SPOT** *see* **CIRCLE**

**SQUARE** 1, 2, 3, 4, 6, 7, 12, 13, 14, 16, 19, 20, 21, 24, 39, 81, 100, 101, 131, 132, 141, 147, 152, 153, 154, 156, 199, 227, 229, 231, 235, 247, 253, 254, 256, 258, 259, 268, 270, 280, 282, 283, 299, 300, 303, 320, 322, 324, 325, 326, 327, 330, 331, 333, 340, 342, 343, 344, 345, 346, 347, 349, 354, 355, 356, 357, 358, 359, 363, 364, 367, 370, 373, 376, 377, 384, 385, 388, 396, 397, 409, 413, 414, 424, 426, 430, 432, 433, 435, 437, 438, 439, 442, 447, 455, 462, 466, 474, 480, 481, 494, 498, 499, 505, 506, 511, 512, 515, 535, 570, 571, 572, 573, 575, 576, 577, 578, 587, 588, 589, 590,

591, 592, 593, 594, 595, 597, 682, 708, 709, 717, 722, 723, 733, 734, 738, 746, 773, 785, 791, 799, 804, 805, 806, 809, 821, 823, 829, 831, 833, 836, 837, 839, 843, 846, 848, 850, 853, 860, 864, 865, 872, 879, 880, 908, 929, 937, 941, 944, 955, 964, 969, 970, 974, 980, 983, 990, 993, 994, 995, 999; *see also* **CHECKERBOARD**

**STAR** 9, 10, 13, 93, 112, 116, 141, 195, 200, 201, 202, 203, 204, 221, 231, 243, 245, 252, 254, 256, 258, 259, 260, 262, 265, 279, 281, 282, 359, 363, 440, 469, 509, 520, 569, 627, 762, 763, 813, 814, 816, 840, 875

**STRIPE** 1, 3, 4, 5, 6, 16, 18, 24, 42, 43, 44, 45, 46, 47, 51, 95, 105, 106, 129, 148, 218, 233, 234, 235, 246, 280, 281, 282, 294, 316, 317, 318, 319, 326, 328, 329, 330, 331, 332, 333, 335, 336, 337, 338, 339, 340, 341, 342, 343, 344, 345, 347, 348, 349, 350, 351, 352, 353, 358, 360, 361, 362, 364, 368, 383, 386, 392, 393, 394, 415, 416, 417, 418, 419, 420, 421, 424, 430, 434, 435, 439, 481, 517, 518, 519, 520, 572, 706, 708, 709, 715, 718, 719, 721, 729, 730, 736, 751, 754, 759, 763, 765, 767, 771, 772, 773, 780, 784, 787, 798, 800, 803, 804, 805, 806, 808, 815, 816, 817, 824, 827, 830, 840, 853, 860, 863, 864, 877, 878, 888, 912, 916, 917, 920, 952, 965, 969, 985, 986, 988, 989, 992, 997, 998

**SWASTIKA/GOOD LUCK SYMBOL** 55, 57, 71, 72, 73, 85, 89, 98, 106, 122, 124, 243, 247, 299, 300, 303, 325, 446, 447, 455, 479

**TARTAN** 587, 588, 589, 590, 591, 592, 593, 594, 595

**TEARDROP** *see* **BOTEH**

**TRIANGLE** 1, 3, 6, 7, 12, 14, 15, 18, 19, 20, 22, 24, 39, 48, 107, 116, 141, 147, 153, 195, 200, 201, 202, 203, 204, 221, 231, 249, 272, 273, 279, 294, 314, 330, 334, 350, 355, 357, 359, 364, 365, 367, 369, 375, 376, 381, 387, 411, 415, 424, 426, 427, 437, 438, 448, 455, 479, 482, 494, 517, 518, 519, 526, 571, 657, 675, 721, 722, 733, 735, 738, 739, 743, 759, 764, 775, 778, 808, 840, 851, 854, 855, 866, 875, 898, 904, 961, 966, 970, 983, 986, 1000

**WAVE** 61, 88, 94, 103, 113, 114, 127, 140, 150, 249, 261, 289, 315, 321, 377, 405, 659, 663, 720, 771, 888; *see also* **SCROLL; SPIRAL; WATER**

**X** *see* **CROSS**

**ZIGZAG** 2, 3, 4, 11, 15, 21, 24, 106, 129, 148, 150, 182, 196, 198, 245, 246, 275, 277, 278, 279, 280, 285, 294, 340, 356, 360, 365, 367, 372, 375, 378, 379, 380, 381, 382, 383, 386, 388, 389, 390, 391, 392, 394, 395, 403, 407, 409, 415, 416, 417, 419, 420, 426, 430, 438, 544, 574, 709, 738, 752, 770, 799, 800, 810, 878, 879, 910, 986, 987, 988

*ZIL-I-SOLTAN* 193, 208, 500

# NATURAL SHAPES

## NATURAL SHAPES *(continued)*

**LEAF (CONTINUED)** 681, 682, 683, 684, 685, 686, 687, 688, 689, 690, 691, 693, 694, 695, 696, 697, 698, 699, 700, 701, 702, 703, 704, 706, 711, 712, 713, 715, 724, 725, 726, 728, 732, 735, 739, 740, 741, 742, 744, 745, 746, 747, 748, 749, 751, 753, 754, 755, 756, 757, 758, 761, 764, 768, 769, 770, 773, 779, 784, 790, 792, 795, 800, 801, 802, 807, 809, 811, 812, 822, 834, 835, 836, 837, 838, 840, 841, 846, 852, 858, 859, 862, 863, 869, 871, 872, 874, 876, 877, 883, 884, 885, 887, 889, 895, 897, 901, 905, 906, 909, 913, 918, 922, 927, 930, 933, 939, 945, 948, 951, 954, 960, 970, 986, 991, 993

**LIGHTNING** *see* **THUNDER**

**MARINE LIFE** 5, 25, 40, 51, 60, 94, 95, 105, 113, 130, 207, 352, 560, 629, 659, 668, 673, 774, 781, 800, 830, 978; *see also* **SHELL**

**MOON** 742

**MOUNTAIN/HILL** 87, 139, 140, 684, 835, 841

**PARTS OF THE BODY** *see* **HUMAN FIGURE**

**REPTILE** 26, 51, 418, 425, 458, 464; *see also* **DRAGON**

**SCIENCE/BIOLOGY** 818, 826, 1000

**SHELL** 521, 555, 556, 560, 562, 728, 782; *see also* **MARINE LIFE**

**SNOW** 87, 122, 139

**SPACE** 842, 886, 896, 957

**SUN** 148, 157, 247, 284, 288, 434, 443, 816, 996

**THUNDER/LIGHTNING** 84, 378, 379, 380, 381, 383, 389, 415, 425, 426

**TREE, GENERAL** 144, 276, 357, 414, 440, 502, 527, 529, 535, 536, 565, 566, 567, 568, 569, 584, 604, 649, 676, 684, 687, 738, 769, 801, 829, 831, 897

**TREE, SPECIFIC: BANANA** 87; **CHESTNUT** 654, 691; **MAPLE** 108, 112, 116, 117, 127, 133, 139; **OAK** 442, 501, 747, 810, 993; **PALM** 287, 288, 291, 293, 440, 566, 742, 770, 811, 985; **PINE** 133, 140, 158; **PLUM** 69; **POMEGRANATE** 233, 237, 239, 255; **SORB-APPLE/SERVICE** 662; **WILLOW** 69

**VEGETABLE** 891

**WATER** 88, 92, 94, 103, 110, 113, 114, 120, 127, 130, 139, 289, 659, 660, 673, 694, 742, 779, 963, 985; *see also* **WAVE**

## MYTHOLOGICAL, RELIGIOUS AND SYMBOLIC

**CHERUB/PUTTO** 209, 296, 515, 521, 528, 529, 543

**CHINESE SYMBOL** 57, 456, 459

**CHRISTIAN SYMBOL** 189, 323, 324, 446, 467, 521, 619

**CIRCLE OF LIFE** 298

**DEITY** 163, 380, 385; *see also* **NAMED DEITIES**

**DRAGON** 51, 59, 60, 61, 62, 130, 450, 464, 479; *see also* **REPTILE**

**KRISHNA** 157

**MIHRAB** 499, 517, 518, 519

**MOTHER EARTH** 145

**MYTHICAL BIRD** 49, 52, 58, 71, 130; *see also* **BIRD**

**NATIVE AMERICAN SYMBOL** 819, 966

**PUTTO** *see* **CHERUB**

**QUR'AN** 207, 214, 359

*SENMURV* *see* **WINGED DOG**

**TAMAR (TALISMAN)** 272, 273, 282

**TREE OF LIFE** 49, 50, 143, 234, 242, 414

**VISHNU** 161

**WHEEL OF LIFE** 161

**WINGED DOG** *(SENMURV)*/**HORSE/LION** 205, 206, 479, 503; *see also* **ANIMAL**

## ARTEFACTS

**ARCHITECTURE** 69, 157, 288, 313, 413, 515, 517, 518, 519, 527, 528, 567, 568, 575, 576, 738, 780, 812, 815, 819, 827, 829, 830, 831, 835, 843, 844, 857, 873, 874, 897, 943, 969, 985

**COSTUME** 35, 69, 138, 156, 157, 163, 180, 181, 292, 296, 385, 407, 427, 428, 429, 467, 521, 524, 525, 527, 528, 529, 534, 543, 550, 558, 568, 780, 812, 828, 830, 831, 832, 833, 834, 835, 837, 841, 873, 900; *see also* **HUMAN FIGURE**

**ELECTRICAL** 827, 839

**HERALDIC DEVICE** 40, 108, 122, 126

**HOUSEHOLD ITEM** 132, 157, 193, 208, 296, 500, 515, 521, 522, 529, 725, 866, 869, 891, 981

**TOOL/WEAPON/INSTRUMENT** 9, 10, 35, 156, 428, 429, 522, 524, 525, 528, 558, 560, 563, 564, 619, 649, 812, 816, 818, 832, 841, 854, 857, 886,

**TRANSPORTATION** 25, 40, 287, 568, 811, 814, 825, 829, 831, 849, 957, 961

## NAMED PERIODS/ART MOVEMENTS

**ART NOUVEAU** 649, 650, 651, 652, 653, 654, 655, 656, 657, 658, 659, 660, 661, 662, 663, 664, 665, 666, 667, 668, 669, 670, 671, 672, 673, 674, 675, 676, 677, 678, 679, 680, 681, 682, 683, 684, 685, 686, 687, 688, 689, 690, 691, 692, 693, 694, 695, 696, 697, 698, 699, 700, 701, 702, 703, 704, 895, 984

**ARTS & CRAFTS** 596, 597, 598, 599, 600, 601, 602, 603, 604, 605, 606, 607, 608, 609, 610, 611, 612, 613, 614, 615, 616, 617, 618, 619, 620, 621, 622, 623, 624, 625, 626, 627, 628, 629, 630, 631, 632, 633, 634, 635, 636, 637, 638, 639, 640, 641, 642, 643, 644, 645, 646, 647, 648

**BAROQUE & ROCOCO** 543, 544, 545, 546, 547, 548, 549, 550, 551, 552, 553, 554, 555, 556, 557, 558, 559, 560, 561, 562, 563, 564

**EARLY 20TH-CENTURY** 31, 32, 33, 37, 45, 46, 121, 129, 158, 160, 240, 241, 243, 244, 246, 247, 248, 289, 292, 326, 331, 332, 333, 334, 338, 341, 361, 364, 437, 438, 439, 573, 705, 706, 707, 708, 709, 710, 711, 712, 713, 714, 715, 716, 717, 718, 719, 720, 721, 722, 723, 724, 725, 726, 727, 728, 729, 730, 731, 732, 733, 734, 735, 736, 737, 738, 739, 740, 741, 742, 743, 744, 745, 746, 747, 748, 749, 750, 751, 752, 753, 754, 755, 756, 757, 758, 759, 760, 761, 762, 763, 764, 765, 766, 767, 768, 769, 770, 771, 772, 773, 774, 775, 776, 777, 778, 779, 780, 781, 782, 783, 784, 785, 786, 787, 788, 789, 790, 791, 792, 793, 794, 795, 796, 797, 798, 799, 800, 801, 802, 803, 804, 805, 806, 807, 808, 809, 810, 811, 812, 813, 814, 815, 816

**MEDIEVAL** 465, 466, 467, 468, 469, 470, 471, 472, 473, 474, 475, 476, 477, 478, 479, 480, 481, 482, 483, 484, 485, 486, 487, 488, 489, 490, 491, 492, 493, 494, 495, 496, 497, 498, 499, 500, 843, 908

**1980s TO THE PRESENT** 30, 42, 43, 93, 99, 100, 128, 139, 140, 179, 354, 355, 381, 384, 385, 410, 411, 414, 415, 418, 421, 422, 423, 424, 985, 986, 987, 988, 989, 990, 991, 992, 993, 994, 995, 996, 997, 998, 999, 1000

**1940s & 1950s** 21, 22, 23, 28, 29, 33, 50, 53, 90, 98, 125, 156, 329, 349, 357, 359, 382, 416, 417, 817, 818, 819, 820, 821, 822, 823, 824, 825, 826, 827, 828, 829, 830, 831, 832, 833, 834, 835, 836, 837, 838, 839, 840, 841, 842, 843, 844, 845, 846, 847, 848, 849, 850, 851, 852, 853, 854, 855, 856, 857, 859, 860, 861, 862, 863, 864, 865, 866, 867, 868, 869, 870, 871, 872, 873, 874, 875, 876, 877, 878, 879, 880, 881, 882, 883, 884, 885, 886, 887, 990

**1960s & 1970s** 18, 19, 20, 21, 22, 23, 383, 413, 888, 889, 890, 891, 892, 893, 894, 895, 896, 897, 898, 899, 900, 901, 902, 903, 904, 905, 906, 907, 908, 909, 910, 911, 912, 913, 914, 915, 916, 917, 918, 919, 920, 921, 922, 923, 924, 925, 926, 927, 928, 929, 930, 931, 932, 933, 934, 935, 936, 937, 938, 939, 940, 941, 942, 943, 944, 945, 946, 947, 948, 949, 950, 951, 952, 953, 954, 955, 956, 957, 958, 959, 960, 961, 962, 963, 964, 965, 966, 967, 968, 969, 970, 971, 972, 973, 974, 975, 976, 977, 978, 979, 980, 981, 982, 983, 984

**19TH-CENTURY** 5, 6, 7, 41, 47, 48, 49, 59, 61, 63, 64, 65, 66, 67, 68, 69, 70, 71, 72, 74, 75–80, 91, 92, 94, 95, 96, 97, 101, 102, 103, 105, 106, 107, 108, 110, 111, 112, 113, 114, 115, 118, 119, 120, 123, 124, 126, 127, 130, 132, 134, 135, 136, 138, 141, 142, 154, 157, 159, 163, 164, 169, 170, 171, 172, 173, 175, 180, 181, 196, 209, 210, 211, 215, 217, 221, 223, 234, 235, 236, 238, 240, 256, 257, 260, 261, 262, 283, 287, 288, 290, 291, 293, 308, 320, 321, 322, 323, 334, 335, 336, 340, 358, 362, 363, 386, 387, 388, 389, 393, 395, 396, 397, 398, 399, 400, 401, 402, 405, 410, 420, 433, 434, 435, 436, 440, 441, 442, 444, 445, 497, 498, 499, 500, 517, 518, 519, 565, 566, 567, 568, 569, 570, 571, 572, 573, 574, 575, 576, 577, 578, 579, 580, 581, 582, 583, 584, 585, 586, 587, 588, 589, 590, 591, 592, 593, 594, 595

**RENAISSANCE** 501, 502, 503, 504, 505, 506, 507, 508, 509, 510, 511, 512, 513, 514, 515, 516, 517, 518, 519, 520, 521, 522, 523, 524, 525, 526, 527, 528, 529, 530, 531, 532, 533, 534, 535, 536, 537, 538, 539, 540, 541, 542

# Introduction

This book is a compilation of patterns from around the world. They have been sourced from archive collections of ceramics, textiles and other decorative surfaces held in museums and by private collectors. Some patterns have been included because they are the highest representation of that area's art available; some are included purely because of their decorative appeal. All are the result of an artist or artisan's desire to produce something of beauty.

Each section of the book runs geographically and includes, where possible, examples from the time before chemical, synthetic dyes were widespread. Efforts have also been made to include patterns that have been produced by hand, by means of painting, embroidery, or weaving.

The majority of the patterns shown are textile designs – either actual examples of the printed or embroidered cloth or the original hand-rendered designs. This is not an unfair bias, and other areas and media are not neglected, but a culture's textiles, more readily portable and affordable than many other media, usually offer us its broadest range of pattern and the fullest realisation of its design skills.

## What is pattern?

Pattern is ubiquitous – we wear it, cover our walls and floors with it, sit on it, eat off it and even sleep on it! Patterns surround us continually as we observe the objects in our world and we begin to see regularity in them. We see pattern in pebbles on a beach, leaves lying on the grass and stars gleaming in the sky. At every moment and on every side, patterns of varying size, colour and definition encircle us. Pattern can be purely ornamental – a pleasing decoration – or it can have enormous religious and cultural significance, saving us from demons and promoting good fortune. Throughout history patterns have used symbolic motifs, specific colours and well-established designs to give meaning and continuity to the messages they contained. Even today, many Eastern countries, in particular, use a restricted colour palette and ancient symbols in their decoration of major buildings. In China, for example, the colours red, green (or gold), white and black dominate their architecture and art. To the Chinese these colours represent more than just their visual richness: each one may also be a compass direction, a season, a quality, an animal and even an emotion.

The dictionary definition of pattern is an ornamental design; we know it best as the recurrence of similar forms at regular intervals. Each ornamental form can be termed a 'motif' and the way in which they regularly occur is called 'the repeat'.

The main lines on which repeats are constructed are few, simple and well established. The art of the surface pattern designer is to arrange them in such a way as to make a pleasing balanced composition in terms of colour, layout and scale – whether for textiles, ceramics or any other decorative surface and to make the resulting design 'fit for purpose'.

A good pattern always has an underlying symmetry. This is necessary for the look and structure of the pattern in its own right and also to fit in with manufacturing requirements – such as the width of a loom or the size of a tile.

## Structure

The simplest of all patterns is the stripe, which is a series of parallel lines that run either horizontally or vertically. Sometimes these are altered to give us the zigzag.

Stripes give a strong directional emphasis whenever they are worn or placed on an interior or exterior surface. For example, we are all familiar with the idea that vertical stripes make the wearer taller or a room seem higher, while horizontal ones make an object seem wider or a ceiling lower. Stripes in both directions give the lattice or grid, which forms the underlying structure for a large number of patterns, such as the tapa designs from Polynesia, which are almost all based upon a basic grid, loosely squared up.

If the angle at which the two lines cross is altered we get the diamond, which is a potent design shape in its own right. However, by introducing a third line and bisecting the diamond laterally, we get an equilateral triangle, which is the basis for an infinity of patterns, using not only the triangle and diamond but also the hexagon, which is six equilateral triangles arranged together.

A fourth series of lines gives the octagon, which forms the basis of yet more radiating patterns. These shapes compounded give the complex, intricate and ingenious variety of patterns we see on tiled, pierced and painted mosque and palace floor, wall and window treatments prevalent throughout the Islamic world because they conform to the Islamic instruction of being geometric in origin.

Many of the above patterns can also be drawn using curved lines and by incorporating circles or arcs. However, the underlying structure is always the square, rectangle, diamond or triangle already described.

It can be observed that certain kinds of ornament are in harmony with a particular type of construction line. For instance, naturalistic forms complement curving free-flowing lines, and formal patterns suit rigid geometric lines. Certain types of design style have centred upon a type of line – for example, patterns of the Art Nouveau movement were based upon a curving sinuous line, while Bauhaus designs are necessarily based upon a rectilinear line.

The characteristic lines of well-established patterns are generally the direct result of the restrictions that the designer has had to abide by. In other words, although certain styles of design may be associated with a particular design period or place, it is almost always the case that a technical or practical reason had to be satisfied. This is generally to do with the methods of production. For instance, the Wiener Werkstätte designs were all block-printed by hand and have the crispness and clarity associated with that method; early engraved roller-printed textiles continued the practice of copperplate printers, who often used images derived from engravings; ceramic patterns have to fit the size of the tile or the shape of object on to which they are to be painted or printed, and so on. As with most endeavours, the practicalities must always be addressed first.

All these patterns, whether for ceramics, textiles or other decorative surfaces are the result of considerable planning and expertise. However, quite often, once a reliable formula has been worked out, it is used over and over again, in endless variations, only changing in colour, texture and dimensions.

Thus, once the pattern has been sketched out, the designer may alter the look of it by means of various devices that make considered use of scale, contrast and texture. An example would be the counterchange, whereby adjacent parts are alternately coloured light and dark. Another device is the turnover, which takes a motif or part of a design and flips it horizontally or vertically. This can form a mirror-repeat or not, depending on the placement. The turnover is a particularly important element in woven textile design and ceramic tiles. The superimposition of one pattern on to another subtler pattern is another well-established device, often used by William Morris in his many surface pattern designs.

## Repeat

For a pattern to be produced by mechanical means, it has to appear to join seamlessly across the width and length of the fabric, paper or wall on to which it is to appear. The process of doing this is termed 'putting the design into repeat' and can often be a highly skilled operation. The finished design must flow well in all directions and should avoid the mechanical effect of too-obvious repetition. Also, it should not show any obvious breaks or distracting areas of pattern, light or shade, as unplanned irregularities may spoil the look of the whole design.

Once the parameters of scale have been decided, the central features of the design can be placed in such a way that they occur next to themselves in a 'side-by-side' repeat. Alternatively, the motifs can be slightly dropped down next to the original placing to give a 'drop' repeat. This can be at half the original length of the main design to give a 'half-drop' repeat, or at lesser or greater intervals, dependent on the desired result. The repeat can also be staggered horizontally, giving a 'brick repeat', most often used in architecture and ceramics.

Patterns that are based on diamonds or the equivalent rounded 'ogee' shapes are known as 'false drops', because they are worked out on square lines and are not dropped at all. A great many late Gothic weaves are designed on this principle.

Another method of repeat is that perfected by weavers in their invention of the sateen weaves, which give rise to 'spot repeats'. This is a system whereby the danger of apparent lines in small repeats is minimised by the careful placing of the motifs in relation to one another. The resulting pattern is often called a 'diaper' pattern and is frequently used in textile designs.

The direction of the repeat is determined by its end use. For instance, wallpaper designs are almost always one-way designs, as are wall tiles. Floor tiles and the majority of apparel (clothing) designs are 'allover' designs, as this serves the manufacturer by not creating wastage. The scale of the design is also dependent on its end use; for example, furnishing designs are generally large, as befits the size of the curtains or large items of furniture that they will cover, while dress designs are usually small or medium in scale, again depending on the area of fabric that will be used and the desired effect. Many designs may be enlarged for one end use or reduced for another.

Textile designs are frequently categorised by the type of ornament that they employ. This traditionally gives us four categories – floral; geometric or abstract; conversational (usually artefacts; literally any object one could have a conversation about); and ethnic. Fashions for and within each category change subtly, giving us, for example, the strong naturalistic and abstracted shapes of the 1950s and 1960s, which mellowed into the quirky and bold abstract designs of the 1970s. Floral designs are the most consistently popular patterns of all.

The use of colour is of paramount importance in pattern design. Today there is an enormous range of colours available, thanks to the inventions of chemists over the last two centuries. Before the 1800s, designers had only natural dyestuffs to work with, which were liable to fade and wash out and required great

skill to use them properly. We have the great Victorian craftsman William Morris to thank for researching and documenting the old methods of dyeing using madder, indigo, weld and other natural dyes. The continued popularity of his designs today means that we can still see examples of these natural dye colours, even if many of his works are now reproduced by chemical means.

The immense range of patterns in this book, drawn from a wide variety of sources and styles, nonetheless all share a geometric underlying structure and the positive aim of delighting the eye of the beholder.

Enjoy!

The patterns in this section are taken from
a wide variety of cultures, covering a time
when artefacts were produced individually and
decorated by hand. Largely produced out of our
need to surround ourselves with items of beauty,
these patterns take their inspiration from the
natural world or the geometric order we impose
on to it. They are often also used as symbols to
ward off impending disaster, and many cultures
used specific motifs and colours for this purpose

– the vane-swastika or good-
luck symbol is a good example
of this practice. Undoubtedly,
the majority of early patterns
were commissioned with this
purpose in mind, and the skill, time and money
invested in their production reflected the status
of the tribe or clan that produced them.
Ordinary working people also wished for
beautiful, auspicious or religiously significant

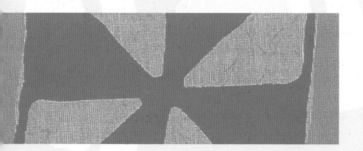

# Part One
# Pre-Industrial

decorations and this is reflected in many of the exquisitely worked embroideries, weaves, prints and painted patterns in this section. In it we find such diverse examples as the convoluted patterns of medieval monks, incredibly detailed designs from the Orient and Near East, patchworks of the early settlers to the United States, and the many woven fabrics that represent hours of labour, collecting, spinning and dyeing the yarn and creating the intricacies of the design. The colours used are often the result of the subtle muted shades of natural dyestuffs; more recent examples use chemical dyes to produce their bright hues. All these patterns are an expression of people's instinctive love of decoration.

*Oceania*

# Polynesia

**1** *Variety is the hallmark of this richly patterned tapa, or siapo, barkcloth from Niue, an island between Tonga and the Cook Islands. The cloth is made from the inner bark of the paper mulberry tree. To create the pattern, the cloth was divided into a primary grid and then subdivided, and the various frames within the subdivisions were then blocked in with freehand designs.*

**2–4** *The zigzag chip-carved designs typically found on Samoan spears and clubs were no doubt an inspiration for these three original Pacific Island patterns. The abstract shapes and plant forms in each pattern have been drawn with a mixture of fine and broad lines, resulting in a satisfying counterbalance between colour and space. An examination of part-finished barkcloths suggests that designs such as these were meticulously worked out to fill the planned grid layout.*

Many of the motifs prevalent throughout the world are said to stem from the Pacific region, especially the eight- or twelve-pointed star shape and the so-called wind vane or vane-swastika or good luck motif. The islands of Polynesia have traditionally used a type of cloth called tapa or barkcloth, which is derived from the inner bark of certain trees. To produce their designs, they are first carved in wood and then transferred to the barkcloth by rubbing over them with dye. They are frequently overpainted by means of a makeshift paintbrush. Often several people at once will have a hand in decorating the tapas. These traditional cloths are used for apparel, ceremonial wear and as general household textiles. They remain some of the few textiles still being made and decorated entirely by hand.

*Oceania*
# Polynesia 2

**5** *Fish are depicted in astonishing detail on this large barkcloth or* ngatu *from Tonga, which dates from the 19th century. To produce the design, the part-dyed cloth was first folded and rubbed with pigment in order to create the guide grid, and then stencilled with the fish motif. Finally, it was overpainted to give emphasis to selected parts of the pattern.*

**6–7** *These two geometric designs, both from the 19th century, are characteristic Fijian cloths that have been decorated by means of a stencil cut from a banana leaf. The technique involves first marking out a grid and then rubbing the stencils with dye, working across the cloth from side to centre until the pattern is complete.*

**8** *A design resembling leaves or pods has been painted freehand on to this barkcloth, or tapa, from Vanuatu. It recalls the patterns found on the island's famous openwork braided mats. Patterned barkcloth is, however, comparatively rare in Vanuatu.*

**9–10** *Pattern design is not a static phenomenon but constantly evolves to reflect new developments and events. Compare these two Fijian cloths: the earlier design, (9), shows spear-like symbols pointing towards a central star. A later cloth, (10), features a stencil-printed muzzle-loading musket motif, complete with trigger guard, ramrod, percussion hammer and surrounding gunshot starbursts.*

7

9

8

10

*Oceania*
# Polynesia 3

**11** *A dominant large zigzag motif is echoed by small zigzag infills in this modern version of a typical Polynesian pattern. Factory-made, it lacks the delightful idiosyncrasies found in hand-printed textiles, but it remains a striking design.*

**12** *Much of the appeal of traditional Polynesian pattern springs from the fact that the village women who printed the designs were able to improvise freely within a basic grid. In this barkcloth, most of the grid squares are blocked out with nine triangles, but the edge contains a line of larger grid squares blocked out with 12 triangles. This out-of-step sequencing makes the pattern vibrant and exciting.*

**13** *Stencils cut from banana leaves were used to produce the 'papercut'-style motifs seen in this pattern. Each leaf stencil was placed within a grid and the coloured pigment then rubbed over it. Once the basic forms of these motifs were in place, the frames were blocked in with colour to give them greater emphasis.*

**14** *The almost three-dimensional effect of this amazingly intricate pattern is due to the way it was produced. First, the cloth was folded, creased and rubbed with pigment so that the guide grid was clearly marked out. Then, each square within the grid was printed by means of a rubbed wooden block; and finally, the whole work was painstakingly overpainted by hand.*

**15** *The serrated pattern that makes up this 20th-century design takes its inspiration from chip carving. This traditional woodworking technique involves using small knives to pattern wood with rows of triangular nicks or chips.*

**16** *Parallel lines with a triangular infill make up this modern woven pattern. The design recalls those seen on ceremonial chip-carved paddle blades and on traditional rub-printed barkcloths.*

**17** *Red, brown and off-white shapes play against each other to form a dynamic, kaleidoscope-like pattern. This liveliness is the result of using two rubbing blocks to print the design. Once a guide grid had been created, the cloth was held taut over a chip-carved and incised wooden block and rubbed with coloured dye. This process was then repeated with the second block. The holes in the block show on the cloth as the unprinted part of the pattern.*

11

12

14

13

15

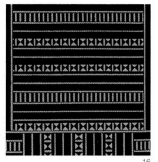
16

*Oceania*

# **Polynesia** 4

**18–20** *Bold and colourful, these patterns straddle two very different cultures. During the 1960s, many Western designers became fascinated by so-called 'primitive' crafts and began to look to ethnic and tribal sources for inspiration. In many cases they simply collected random batches of ethnic fabrics and lifted the designs directly from the pattern. The two 1960s patterns on the left (18 and 19) and the pattern in the centre (20) are clearly motifs that have been taken from a Polynesian source, almost certainly a barkcloth. They have, however, been somewhat 'tidied up' in order to suit Western silk-screen printing techniques. The large pattern in the centre (20) is particularly interesting: with its clean lines and jumping colour counterchange it is a typical example of a 1960s printed fabric, but there is no denying that at its heart it is a Polynesian pattern.*

18

19

**21–23** The three patterns on the right – all characteristic examples of printed patterns that were produced in the West in the 1950s and 1960s – draw their inspiration from traditional Polynesian barkcloths. This is borne out by the use of the figure of eight motif, the heavily stylised flowers, the zigzag pattern infill and the colour-block counterchange set within a grid. As to why Western designers were so happy to copy the designs, the answer has to do with the way the original Polynesian cloths were printed. When Western designers saw how the patterns had been produced by stretching barkcloth over carved blocks and then rubbing colours through – a printing technique that resulted in a design of one or more colours on a white ground – they immediately realised that, with a minimum of design effort, they could produce much the same patterns using modern silk-screen presses.

21

20

22

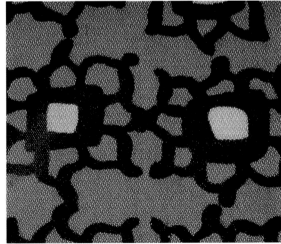

23

24

25

26

27

# Southeast Asia
# Indonesia

**24** *Made in Sumatra, this sumptuous woven silk sari has been created by first setting up the loom for a plain weave and then by hand-brocading gilt weft threads into the plain warp. The richness of the pattern suggests that it was made for a special ceremonial occasion.*

**25** *A charming sarong made using the batik technique. This involves repeatedly wax-printing a resist design on a plain woven cloth, dipping the cloth in dye so that the waxed areas resist the colour, and then ironing to remove the wax.*

**26** *This Javanese sarong depicts a collection of animals that were thought to have mystical powers. The boldness of the design suggests that it is a man's sarong.*

**27** *The imagery of birds and flowers on this sarong – swallows and ears of corn or rice – and the way that the images are placed tells us that it was designed to be worn by a mature married woman.*

The majority of the printed patterns in this section derive from Java, which has a long and rich tradition of decorating cloths for apparel, ritual or domestic purposes. Cloths are woven from cotton or silk and decorated using a carefully drawn or blocked pattern of molten beeswax that resists the dyes. The vibrant colours shown here are often chemical dyes, but all cloths produced before the beginning of the 19th century would have used vegetable or mineral dyes. The choice of colour is related to the age and perceived status of the recipient with pastel colours being used for the young, full reds and blues for the mature woman and greys, purples and darker colours for older patrons. The batiks use motifs that have symbolic meanings or are stylised naturalistic forms, sometimes drawn in the European style for the Western market.

*Southeast Asia*
# Indonesia 2

**28** *A beautiful batik floral sarong made in the Peranakan style in Java, by Oey Soe Tjoen Kedoengwoeni, sometime about 1950. The pattern was created by hand-drawing a wax resist on to a plain machine-woven cotton cloth. The colour counterchange design, with its characteristic butterfly-and-bouquet motif, is a special feature of the artist's work.*

**29** *Signed 'Pekalonga', this fine batik sarong bears the stamped mark of Geo. Wehry & Co. This tells us that it was made in Java for a Dutch trading firm sometime in the 1950s. The sarong was designed to be worn by a mature married woman: the motif of small chicks is a characteristic 'code', designed to tell the world that the wearer was a prosperous lady with plenty of grandchildren.*

**30** *The batik artist Oey Soe Tjoen Kedoengwoeni drew inspiration from Chinese designs for this cotton cloth, made in Java in the 1980s. The arrangement of the patterns and motifs suggests that the cloth was designed not to be worn as a sarong but rather to be hung on the wall like a tapestry.*

**31** *This high-cost, top-quality batik cotton sarong was made in Java by Lies van Zuylen, an Indo-European artist, sometime between 1900 and 1910. The way the hand-drawn wax resist was painstakingly spaced so that it filled the available ground made it expensive to produce. The high price and the use of late summer flowers within the motifs tells us that this cloth was designed to be worn by a prosperous middle-aged Indo-European woman.*

28

29

**32** *Designed and produced for the local market, this batik sarong was made in Java in 1937 by Lies van Zuylen. The motifs on cloths of this type and character had little or no significance, other than to suggest that the wearer was delicate and refined.*

**33** *During World War II, square batik appliqués such as this were produced in Indonesia for officers of the occupying Japanese army. This example was made in Java in 1943. It is likely that the army officers specially requested the use of the chrysanthemum motif, a Japanese symbol of long life and happiness. The glazed silklike finish was achieved by burnishing the cloth with a wine bottle.*

30

31

32

33

*Southeast Asia*

# Indonesia

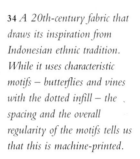

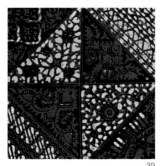

**34** *A 20th-century fabric that draws its inspiration from Indonesian ethnic tradition. While it uses characteristic motifs – butterflies and vines with the dotted infill – the spacing and the overall regularity of the motifs tells us that this is machine-printed.*

**35** *The designer of this machine-printed fabric has chosen a seemingly traditional Indonesian motif. Shadow puppets, however, have little connection with traditional Indonesian textiles.*

**36** *This detail comes from a beautifully handworked Javanese batik sarong. The overall design reflects the batik workers' view of their universe: in the upper world (seen here) there are birds and flying creatures, and in the lower world fish and serpents.*

**37** *This sarong, made in the first decade of the 20th century, dates to a time when pressure for increased production from* Chinese and European traders *began to affect the shape of the patterns and motifs. Village women who once made the batiks for pleasure now did the process in a rush, with the effect that the images are less defined.*

**38** *This Javanese sarong is a wonderful example of canting work. Wax is broken into small pieces and put into a long-spouted brass canting – rather like a miniature kettle. The canting is heated and the liquid wax is trailed over the cloth to mark out the lines of the design. The cloth is then dipped into the dye and finally ironed to remove the wax.*

**39** *A mix of block printing and wax trailing was used to make this modern batik cloth. The ground was divided into a square grid and then subdivided to create triangles within squares within squares. The small squares were worked with a block dipped in wax, and finally the whole design overworked with trailed wax.*

**40** *This wax-trailed Javanese batik sarong was most likely intended as a wedding gift. This is borne out by the inclusion of motifs relating to clan prosperity: cockerels for male virility, ships for abundance, and a heraldic motif or coat of arms for the groom's family.*

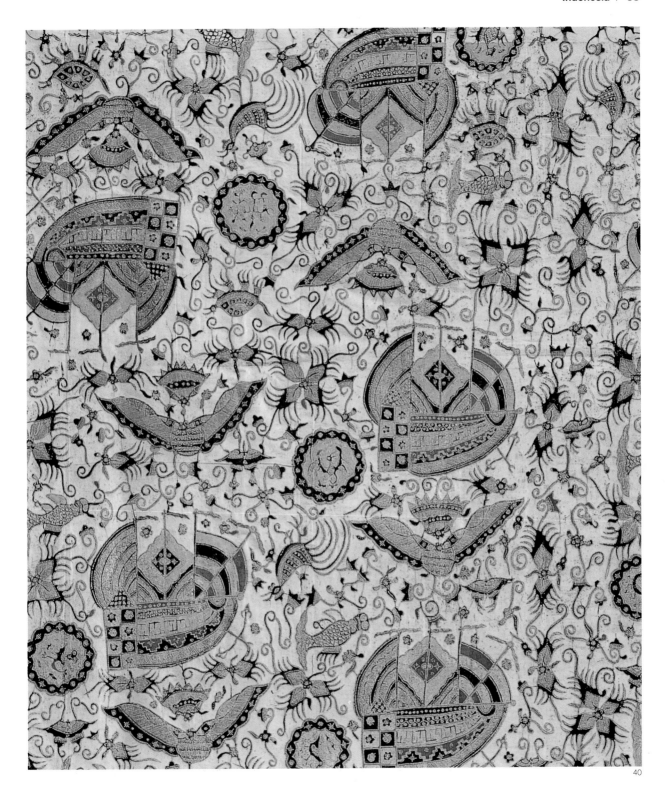

*Southeast Asia*
# Indonesia 4

**41** *A woven cloth made in Western Indonesia in the last quarter of the 19th century. While the strong flower-like motifs point to this being a woven ikat cloth, the crispness of the outlines belies the fact and suggests that this cloth was possibly created by a technique of adding weft strands to an otherwise plain warp.*

**42** *Offered as a funeral gift, this woven sapang or shoulder cloth dates from the 1980s. It was made in the town of Ngada in Flores, a region famous for its supplementary weft cloths. This technique involves painstakingly adding brightly coloured weft threads to an otherwise plain cloth.*

**43** *On a blue-black ground, a variety of geometrical motifs float between lines of brightly coloured weft. Sarongs of this type are one-sided: on the plain side, the weft motifs only show as small dashes or picks of weft thread floating over the warp. This woven sarong was made in the Manggarai region of Flores in the early 1980s.*

**44** *While this sarong was made in Sumatra using ikat techniques – meaning the warp threads were tied and dyed before being woven – the strength of the colours and their unusual arrangement suggest that the weaver drew inspiration from outside influences, perhaps from the Philippines.*

41

42

43

44

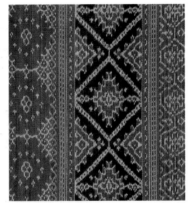

45

**45** *Ikat cloths are characterised by the motifs being blurred in the direction of the warp – or you might say there appears to be a colour bleed that runs parallel to the length of the cloth. This woven ikat cloth was made in the Sikka region of Flores in the early 20th century.*

**46** *A hand-trailed, wax-resist Javanese sarong made in the first quarter of the 20th century. This characteristic design is known as* parang rusak, *meaning a broken dagger-like rock. Legend has it that it was created by the Sultan Agung, the first Muslim ruler. The story tells how he drew inspiration from the jagged rocky coasts of the region.*

**47** *Autumn-flowering chrysanthemums are framed by an outer border of lilies on this Javanese sarong. The subtle, rather quiet, colours of this piece tell us that it was designed for an older woman. The cloth was made by Lien Metzelar in the last years of the 19th century.*

46

47

*Southeast Asia*

# Indonesia 5

**48** *The triangular forms used on this late 19th-century Javanese batik sarong reflect the traditional northern Javanese style of much older block-printed forms. In this example, the classic form has been mixed with modern animal motifs to create a high-quality prestigious cloth.*

**49** *The traditional 'Sawat' (large wings) motif found on this Javanese batik waistcoat (probably dating to the 19th century) represents the Tree of Life and the garuda – a bird-like creature from Hindu-Javanese mythology that carried Vishnu through the heavens.*

**50** *The vertical direction of the blur within the stylised birds and Tree of Life motif on this 1940s ikat indicates a warp ikat – meaning the warp threads were organised and then tied and dyed, all before they were mounted on the loom.*

**51** *While the cloth from this sarong is Indonesian, the motifs, dragons, snakes and shrimps, all derive from Chinese traditions. The weaver has used two techniques, a floating weft for the white dragons and a tied-and-dyed ikat weft for the motifs on the red ground.*

**52** *The large motifs in this example are the stylised wings of the garuda – a mythical bird*

*– while the 'sprouting' or 'growing' motifs represent fertility. This particular design is one of the 'forbidden' patterns, from a time in the 18th century when the sultans decreed that certain patterns were banned to commoners.*

**53** *Traditionally there were patterned cloths for each and every occasion – weddings, births and funerals for example. In the 1940s, however, when there was a shortage of cloth, the printers developed multipatterned cloth featuring stylised flowers and foliage, which could be worn for just about every occasion.*

48

49

51

50

52

54

55

56

57

## East Asia
# China

**54** *The flowing patterns on this vase were created using a technique similar to cloisonné work. Heavy-bodied glaze is trailed over the part-fired pot so that the primary lines of the design stand up in slight relief.*

**55** *Tessellating patterns of this type are found all over the Far East. The never-ending pattern is made up of a single motif – colour counterchanged and mirror reversed – that has a swastika or good luck symbol at its heart.*

**56** *On this woven silk fabric the stylised bats symbolise longevity and the butterflies happiness. The everlasting knot – a motif that seems to cross time, space and cultures – symbolises eternity.*

**57** *A woven and embroidered fabric comprising naturalistic bamboo stems to signify youth and long life, and cherry blossoms for beauty. Interspersed is a stylised chi symbol for good luck; note the miniature swastikas within the chi symbol.*

China has a long and honourable tradition of exquisite pattern-making in all the decorative arts, including textiles, ceramics and painting. Many of the motifs used have a special relevance to the diverse Chinese cultures and religions or derive from ancient Chinese mythology. Favourable emblems such as cranes, phoenixes, peonies and plum blossoms are regularly used to ensure good luck, prosperity, happiness and longevity. For maximum effect, they are often depicted with Chinese characters, such as chi, signifying life and energy. One of the most potent symbols in Chinese pattern-making is the dragon. This fearsome beast is found in many guises, but always exemplifies male power and yang energy. The constant appurtenance of the dragon is a ball, variously interpreted as the sun, the moon or the pearl of potentiality.

## East Asia
# China 2

58

58 *A silk-and-gilt-thread, tapestry-woven mirror case made in the mid-17th century. At the centre of the design is a characteristic mythical bird: the phoenix or feng. The phoenix is a female symbol that promises a bounteous harvest and a prosperous ripeness – a perfect wedding gift.*

59 *Symbolic motifs abound in this 19th-century fabric. The dragon represents male strength and vitality, peonies and clouds symbolise a harmonious future and butterflies stand for marital bliss and fidelity.*

*The gold background indicates that the fabric was intended for the emperor or one of his descendants.*

60 *Made sometime in the middle of the 18th century, this exquisitely embroidered silk hanging is said to have hung in the Imperial Palace. This story is borne out by the embroidery's subject matter – the five dragons with the pearl at the centre – and the fact that the motifs are worked on a gold ground. Yellow or gold was known as the colour of control and was reserved for the emperor and his descendants.*

59

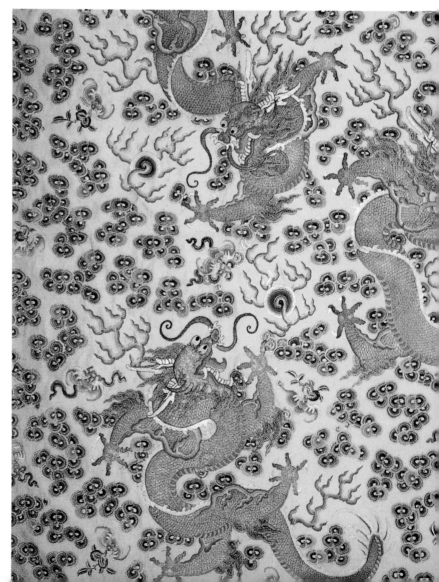

**61** 'Slit tapestry' is the weaving technique used to create this silk fabric. If you look at the pattern closely you will see how, with the warp running along the length of the cloth, the pattern was achieved by running weft threads across the width of the warp. The slits mark the point in the block of colour where an individual weft thread loops around a warp thread to make its return journey. This fragment comes from a garment, possibly a cuff or band, made in the mid-19th century at the time of the Ching dynasty.

**62** The use of the chi-lin (Chinese unicorn) motif set on a gold ground tells us that this garment was part of the ceremonial regalia. It was probably worn by a high-ranking official, possibly an imperial son-in-law. This embroidered silk-and-gilt-thread cloth was made sometime at the beginning of the 17th century.

61

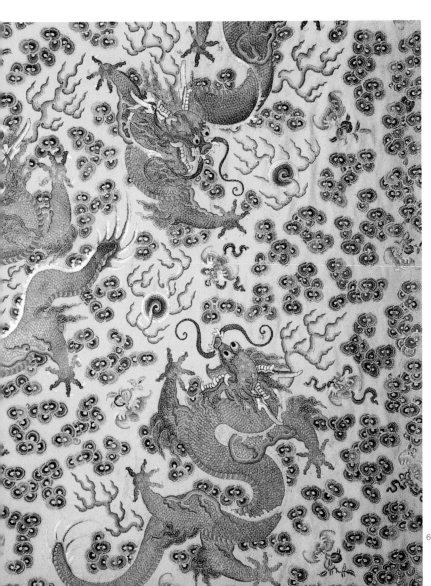

62

*East Asia*
# China 3

63

64

**63** *'Chinoiserie' – the taste
for decoration based on Chinese
design – was immensely popular
in Europe during the 19th century.
This late 19th-century wallpaper,
featuring stylised peonies, draws
its inspiration from an early
19th-century Chinese vase.*

**64** *A mid-19th-century European
interpretation of an earlier 19th-
century Chinese design. When
European designers saw patterns
and motifs of this character, they
stripped them from their original
context and used them in every
kind of application, from wallpapers
and fabrics to endpapers for books.*

**65–68** *These mid-19th-century English designs all draw their inspiration from high-quality contemporary Chinese ceramics which had been plundered from public buildings during the Ti-Ping Opium War rebellions. These pieces were very different from items made solely for export, which up to that time had accounted for nearly all of the Chinese objects collected in Europe and America. English designers found them to be 'truly harmonious in colour and form'. Many of these Chinese designs were quickly born again as English tiles, furnishings and wallpapers. When we now see motifs and patterns of this type we don't immediately think of them as being Chinese; rather, we tend to regard them as prime examples of 19th-century English design – imagery that we associate with Victorian designers such as William Morris.*

65

67

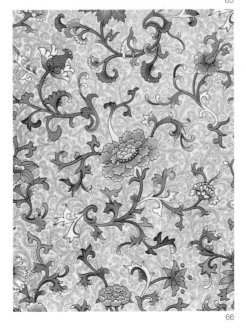
66

68

*East Asia*
# China 4

**69** *Plum and willow trees, pagodas, figures in traditional Chinese dress crossing a bridge – these are all elements of what came to be known as 'willow pattern'. This 19th-century English textile takes its inspiration from earlier Chinese patterns and motifs. With its stylised imagery, drawn in the Western manner, it is a typical example of 'chinoiserie'.*

**70** *This English frieze pattern, drawn in the middle of the 19th century, was inspired by the decoration on*

*an early 19th-century Chinese bottle. In England, patterns of this type came to be used generally on wallpapers and pottery.*

**71** *Two classic Chinese motifs, the phoenix and the cloud, provided the inspiration for this 19th-century textile. Probably French in origin, the cloth comprises embroidery on a woven ground. If you look closely you will see that the maze-like background pattern is made of interlocking swastikas, another Chinese motif.*

69

70

71

72

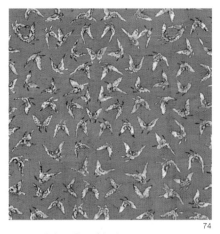

74

**72** *Drawn by Albert Charles Racinet in the early 1870s, this pattern takes its inspiration from a Chinese fabric. While the six-pointed flower motif has been so heavily stylised that it is barely recognisable as Chinese, the underlying pattern of interlocking swastikas is beautifully drawn. The colours and the arrangement of motifs suggest that the fabric was possibly part of the lining of a robe or jacket.*

**73** *This pattern has been taken from a large Chinese jar executed in cloisonné enamel. The technique involves soldering thin metal wires or strips on to a copper base to form little pockets. When these pockets are filled with glaze or enamel and fired, the colours melt to form brilliant ponds of colour.*

**74** *A mass of stylised butterflies – symbols of wedded bliss – are worked in gilt-thread tapestry upon a finely woven pale blue silk ground. The pattern decorates a 19th-century woman's garment, possibly a costly semi-formal robe.*

73

*East Asia*
# China 5

75

77

79

76

78

80

**75–83** *Nine illustrations by Owen Jones, taking details and motifs directly from fine Chinese porcelain. Brilliantly coloured Chinese pieces attracted particular attention in the West at the Great London Exhibitions of 1851 and 1855; the details here were published in Jones's book,* The Grammar of Ornament, *in 1856. Although the more basic blue-and-white Chinese wares had long been familiar to Western audiences, the forms of Chinese art were not widely understood and were crudely and unsympathetically imitated on cheap china throughout Europe. The designs here include a pomegranate, symbolic of fertility and in Chinese art nearly always shown partially open to reveal its seeds; the lotus, an emblem of purity and one of the 'eight treasures' of Buddhism, held in particular reverence in China; and a relatively naturalistic interpretation of the double gourd, a motif that often appears in a more formalised shape to symbolise the pairing of heaven and*

81

82

84

83

85

**84** *Known as 'Kaminari' (the Japanese word meaning thunderbolts), this motif is taken from a Chinese vase dating to the Heian period – the Japanese historical era 794–1185, when there were active trade relations between Japan and China. The square eddy in the form of a border indicates a thunderbolt, which in turn symbolises strength and power.*

**85** *This particular design is made up of a whole number of propitious symbols. Within the diamonds that encircle the royal flower, there are arranged and complete swastikas (a Buddhist symbol or mark of good fortune denoting happiness, benevolence or an act of charity). Every part of the design is conveying messages that carry a symbolic strengthening of well-being.*

*earth. The motifs are beautifully rendered and the colours are clean, bright, pure and delicate. Even Jones, who was surprisingly not a fervent admirer of Chinese art, admitted that 'the Chinese are certainly colourists, and are able to balance with equal success both the fullest tones of colour and the most delicate shades'.*

86

# East Asia
# Japan

**86** *Wisteria flowers trail against a stylised fretted bamboo screen. This detail comes from the outer garment of a typical Noh theatrical female costume, dating from the late 18th century.*

**87** *A detail from a modern hand-painted, stencil-dyed bingata pattern. The banana trees and the snow-capped mountains are created by a mix of brush and stencil techniques. The clear, crisp-edged colours are typical of the bingata technique.*

**88** *The stylised wave is a favourite Japanese motif. Here it is used in a multicolour repeat pattern on a characteristic woven hira ori or silk-brocaded panel.*

**89** *Stylised bamboo motifs are set against a swastika maze in this modern Japanese fabric, which has been designed to imitate a much older embroidered and woven silk fabric. In Kabuki theatre, the swastika symbolises strength when worn by a man, and a sinister character when worn by a woman.*

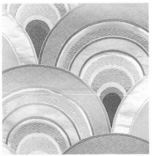

87

88

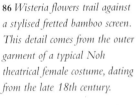

89

The motifs traditionally found in Japanese patterns – such as bamboo, plum blossom, clouds and butterflies – are a celebration of the natural world. But Japanese designs do not merely depict nature: motifs are nearly always chosen for their symbolic meaning, for instance prosperity, happiness or long life. The kimono, with its standardised shape and expanse of fabric, offers a superb 'blank canvas' for pattern makers to demonstrate their artistry, while the costumes of classical Noh or popular Kabuki theatre also show off the designer's skill. Traditional pattern-making techniques include *shiboru* (sewn tie-dyeing) and various paste-resist methods, some using stencils and others applied freehand. A number of avant-garde Japanese designers today are adapting traditional techniques in innovative ways.

*East Asia*
# Japan

**90** Bamboo, plum flower and cloud motifs are printed on a twill silk fabric. This detail comes from an underkimono made in the mid-20th century.

**91** Found in a late 19th-century pattern album, this piece of cloth comprises a rice-paste resist design on a length of woven silk, with added silk embroidery. The scrolling flower design draws inspiration from the paulownia flower, a motif popular during the Edo period.

**92** A detail from a piece of bast or asa fibre, possibly hemp (linen) – a cloth favoured by the nobility – showing a stencilled chrysanthemum flower motif.

The cloth dates from the late 19th century and was made in Okinawa in the Ryukyu Islands. When viewed in its totality the pattern suggests a pond scene – chrysanthemums and lilies against rippled waters.

**93** The colourful silk kimono from which this detail is taken shows a garden in full bloom, set against a decorative curtain or screen. It was made in Kyoto in the last quarter of the 20th century. The design was achieved by a technique known as yuzen, meaning that it was hand-painted with resist pastes and then dyed.

92

90

91

93

94

95

96

94 *This detail is taken from a 19th-century kimono belonging to the famous Kabuki actor Ichikawa Danjuro. The carp motif and the stylised waves, complete with a flaming sceptre tail, are symbols of good luck and achievement – just right for an actor.*

95 *The blurred edging to the lucky carp motif suggests that the design was created using a technique like ikat. This involves tying and dyeing the warp yarn before mounting it on the loom for weaving. This section detail comes from a length of woven bast or asa fabric – a linen-like cloth – made in the late 19th century.*

96 *An illustrated detail – gouache on paper – from* The Grammar of Chinese Ornament, *a pattern book published in the 19th century by Owen Jones. This design, though originally borrowed from China, has been part of Japanese art since Heian times (794–1185).*

97 *Cranes are considered to be an auspicious symbol in Japan, likely to bring good fortune and long life. In this late 19th-century bedding cover they are set in a roundel motif and used as stencilled decoration on a woven ground.*

97

*East Asia*
# Japan 3

**98** Stylised bamboo, plum flower and cloud motifs dominate this pattern, which also features an underlying swastika maze. It is part of a woven figured silk underkimono, made in the late 1940s. Bamboo is a symbol of hard work and fortitude.

**99** A section from a silk kimono, made in 1990 by the renowned textile printer Matsubara Yoshichi.

This design, called 'Flight', was created by using a sequence of 29 'window' stencils of increasingly smaller size, with rice-paste resist and repeated dippings in indigo dye. The cloth's dark blue colour is the result of all 29 dippings, while the little dash of white represents the undyed shape of the last stencil in the sequence.

98

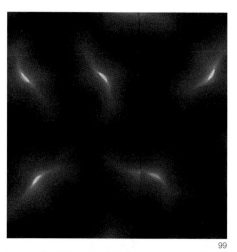

99

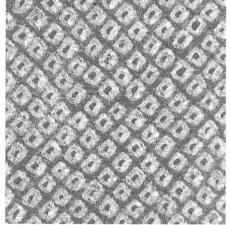

100

**100** *The distinguished artist-designer Itachiku Kubota made this tie-dye cloth in the late 20th century. The pattern was created by sewing and binding the cloth and dipping it in dye – a technique that results in the characteristic* hitta *or repeat-square design. The Japanese tie-dye technique is known as* shiboru, *meaning to squeeze or twist.*

**101** *This resist-dyed and woven cotton bedcover dates from the late 19th century. The pattern was created by grouping the yarn to make the warp, then binding and dyeing the resultant warp hank so that the bindings resist the dye, and finally mounting the resultant multiblue warp on the loom and throwing across the weft.*

**102** *The motifs featured in this robe pattern – cranes, clouds, and chrysanthemums – are all characteristic propitious symbols of prosperity, long life and happiness. According to Japanese myth, cranes are thought to live for a thousand years. The robe was made from bast – a linen-like fibre – in Okinawa in the Ryukyu Islands, during the late 19th century.*

**103** *An illustrated detail taken from a woven and printed kimono, painted in the 19th century. The design features a stylised chrysanthemum – a symbol of happiness – set in a sea of stylised waves. In the autumn the Japanese enjoy a pastime called 'chrysanthemum viewing'.*

**104** *The design of this modern fabric draws its inspiration from falling cherry, peach and plum blossom, set against a blue sky. Possibly the work of a student, it has been silk-screen-printed on a woven cotton ground. If you look closely at the design you should be able to spot the repeat that defines the edge of the printing screen.*

101

103

102

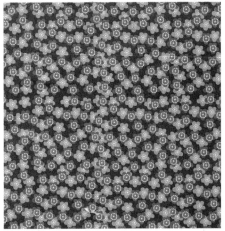

104

*East Asia*
# Japan 4

**105** Mulberry paper stencil plates such as this are used in traditional Japanese fabric printing. After the fragile paper stencil has been cut, a fine grid pattern of thin silk threads is glued in place across the stencil so that it stays in one piece. This stencil plate dates from the 19th century.

**106–108** Three 19th-century illustrations, gouache on paper, showing details from 17th- and 18th-century fabrics, painted by Auguste Racinet for his famous pattern book L'Ornement polychrome. The illustration at bottom right (**108**) is intriguing, in that it bears a clan or family crest badge. Such cloths were sometimes

105

107

106

108

used as shop curtains to indicate that they were open for business. In symbol and form, the components that make up the crest badge motif – the maple leaves set in a bamboo roundel – would have spelled out the family name. The bottom left pattern (**106**) is one version of the many designs that originate from the swastika, a Buddhist symbol meaning happiness, benevolence or an act of charity. In Edo times the swastika was a mark of good fortune.

**109** The much-loved Japanese motif of the chrysanthemum is the main feature of this design, which features on a modern

woman's obi or sash. The use of the chrysanthemum suggests that this is a garment designed for autumn wear.

**110** Made in the Ryukyu Islands, this late 19th-century cotton robe is patterned with a stencilled design. The maple leaves and bamboos were traditionally considered to be appropriate for a woman's early summer or autumn kimono, designed to be worn to view the foliage in Kyoto.

**111** A detail from an early 19th-century bast or linen-like kimono, stencil-printed, with silk embroidery. The use of the iris flowers with the rippled water suggests that this is a kimono for summer wear.

**112** A detail from a 19th-century bedcover or a futon, printed using the rice-paste resist technique and painted with a carp roundel. The carp symbolises long life and achievement.

**113** Paste-resist decoration is here combined with embroidery on a pattern-woven ground. The design features paulownia and chrysanthemum flowers against a backdrop of clouds. This late summer or autumn kimono was made sometime in the second quarter of the 20th century.

109

111

113

110

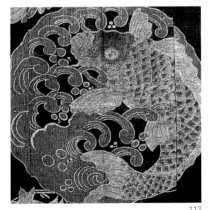

112

*East Asia*
# Japan 5

114

115

116

117

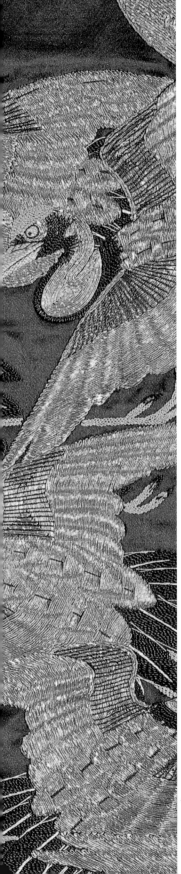

114 *This beautifully detailed design has been embroidered with silk and metallic thread upon a woven silk ground. The detail is from a kimono made in the mid-19th century. The use of the paired ducks – symbolising happiness and harmony – suggests that this may have been part of a wedding outfit.*

115 *A section of* komon *– meaning a small crest or pattern – fabric made towards the end of the 19th century. The komon technique involves punching holes through paper to make a stencil, spreading a rice-paste resist through the stencil plates on to cotton cloth, and then dyeing the cloth a single colour.*

116 *A stylised hemp-leaf motif is arranged upon a background lattice derived from the maple leaf. This luxurious silk brocade comes from a Noh costume for a nobleman's hunting cloak, made during the Edo period (1603–1868).*

117 *Gift-wrapping is important in Japanese culture, and this modern mass-produced wrapping paper draws its inspiration from a pot-pourri of traditional designs. Note the stylised irises, the maple leaves and the flower blossoms, all symbols related to good luck and happiness.*

118 *Golden cranes – a symbol of longevity – fly upon a blue background. This early 19th-century bedcover, with silk-and-metallic-thread embroidery on a woven silk ground, would have been a wedding gift.*

119 *Inspired by Chinese porcelain designs, this pattern of linked clouds is a symbol of changing fortune. The detail is from a late 19th-century woven-silk Noh theatrical robe.*

120 *A detail from a late 19th-century fabric, embroidered silk on a woven silk ground. The meandering water pattern is still used for* yukata *– meaning block-printed cloth – in the traditional summer colours of blue on white.*

119

120

118

*East Asia*
# Japan 6

**121** *Bright and colourful, this design features butterflies and peonies – motifs that symbolise well-being and prosperity. The pattern is printed on a silk ground and is taken from a 1930s sample book.*

**122** *A detail from a late 18th-century kimono, stencil-dyed with silk-and-metallic-thread embroidery on a woven figured silk ground. The design features hollyhock and paulownia flowers ringed by snowflakes. The hollyhock was adopted as the Tokugawas' (a group of famous shoguns) personal pattern or crest.*

**123** *The peony motif, a favourite flower of the Edo period, was loved for its bright freshness. Here it decorates a kimono made in the middle of the 19th century. The fabric uses the rice-paste resist-dye technique combined with silk and metallic embroidery on a woven figured silk ground.*

**124** *A section from an early 19th-century kimono, dyed and embroidered on a woven silk ground, featuring peony flowers set on a swastika pattern. This version of the peony motif has its origins in ancient China, and because it was used in conjunction with the swastika (a Buddhist symbol meaning happiness) the kimono was most probably a wedding gift.*

121

124

122

125

123

126

**125** *A chrysanthemum pattern has been applied on a bast or linen ground using rice-paste resist. This technique – also called* tsutsugaki – *involves brushing paste through a stencil and dipping the cloth in a cold vegetable dye. The detail comes from a mid-20th-century bedcover.*

**126** *A 19th-century gouache-on-paper illustration. This is a reinterpretation of a family crest. Edo versions of this design were used to decorate everyday objects, like the* furoshiki, *or body cloth, used by bathers at the public baths.*

**127** *A detail from a late 19th-century child's robe, with stencilled decoration on a bast or linen cloth ground. The stylised ducks, irises, maple leaves and the meandering stream symbolise happiness and unity, perfect for a child's clothing.*

**128** *This late 20th-century* obi *or kimono sash was created using the* yuzen *technique. The outlines were painted with paste resist and then the enclosed areas were blocked in with the colour. The use of the red and white camellias points to this being part of a winter outfit.*

127

128

*East Asia*
# Japan 7

**129** *Each of the hexagonal panels in this fabric tells a story. The wavy stripes at top right, for example, describe spring cherry blossom. Silk embroidery on a woven silk ground was used to create this early 20th-century* obi *or sash.*

**130** *A detail from a mid-19th-century sample book. Within the stylised waves, there are dragons, crabs, carp, phoenixes, deer and seaweed – all traditional motifs that symbolise long life and well-being.*

**131** *This modern cloth features a* rasen *or radial pattern. The design was achieved by a method known as* shiboru, *meaning to wring or squeeze. This tie-dye technique involves pinching and gathering the cloth, binding it with fine string and immersing it in a vat of cold vegetable dye.*

**132** *A section from a length of late 19th-century woven* kasuri *or* ikat *cloth featuring a flower in the shape of a cross and a vase of plum blossom, symbolising charm and*

129

innocence. The combination of
these symbols suggests that this
is a pattern for a child's garment.

**133** *Stylised maple leaves, cherry
blossom, pine needles and pine
cones all feature on this design.
The motifs suggest that this is
a garment for spring wear. The
pattern was stencil-dyed on an
indigo-dipped ground. The detail
is from a* furisode *(a coat-like
garment) made in the Edo
period (1603–1868).*

**134** *A detail from a 19th-century
kimono, ikat-dyed and woven from
bast – a linen-like plant fibre. The
pattern features chrysanthemums,
a motif favoured for celebration and
festival wear.*

**135** *Bamboo and wisteria motifs
make up the pattern on this 19th-
century paper stencil plate. It was
designed to be used in a technique
known as* katazome, *which
involves spreading a rice-paste resist
through a stencil and dipping the
resultant cloth in a cold dye vat.*

130

133

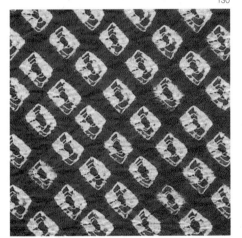

131

134

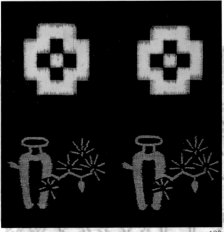

132

135

*East Asia*
# Japan 8

**136** *Costumes decorated with peach and plum blossom were worn in Japan for high days, holidays and weddings. This detail comes from a late 19th-century kimono. It is of woven figured silk with a flowering plum design – a symbol of charm and innocence.*

**137** *Chrysanthemum, iris and peony flowers are arranged on a herringbone brick-lattice ground. The pattern is embroidered in silk thread on a woven figured silk ground. This detail comes from an 18th-century Noh theatrical robe and the design is closely linked with the traditional patterns of the Kabuki theatre.*

**138** *A section from a length of delicate crêpe-weave silk, with stencilled decoration, made in the 19th century in Okinawa on the Ryukyu Islands. The design features plum blossom and umbrellas – both motifs favoured by the Ryukyu aristocracy.*

**139** *Look closely at this pattern and you will see a great number of traditional Japanese motifs, including maple leaves, ivy leaves, peony flowers, rippled waters, hillsides and snow. The detail is taken from a piece of late 20th-century Japanese gift-wrapping paper.*

136

137

138

140

**140** *The dynamic wavy line pattern seen here, complete with mountains, floating clouds and pine forests, is a modern Japanese reinterpretation of an old Japanese design. This detail comes from a late 20th-century kimono. It is stencil printed using the* katazome *technique on a woven silk ground.*

**141** *Executed in gouache on paper, this is a 19th-century European artist's reinterpretation of a traditional Japanese pattern. The basket-weave design draws inspiration from* ajiro, *a type of traditional braided bamboo basketry. The* ajiro *weave was used for everything from ceiling construction to fishing nets.*

**142** *A section from an obi, a kimono sash, made in the mid-19th century, woven using a* nishiki *or brocade-like technique. Chrysanthemum, plum and peach blossom motifs were favoured for special spring and summer celebrations, weddings and festivals.*

141

139

142

143

## South Asia
# India & Pakistan

*143 A vibrant embroidered silk fabric on a woven silk ground from a skirt made in Gujarat. The design features a number of typical Indian motifs, such as tulips, flowers of the Tree of Life, and the peacock for fertility and happiness.*

144

*144 In the 1770s French soldiers in Egypt discovered 'Eastern' shawls and sent them home as gifts. As a result, woven Kashmiri shawls such as this – which dates from the 18th century – became coveted fashion accessories in Europe.*

145

*145 A hanging for a shrine, of embroidered cotton on a woven cotton ground. The rows of sacred cows symbolise the fertility of the earth.*

*146 The design on this skirt features the* boteh, *a motif used right across India and Asia. It is a symbol of fecundity indicating fertility, creativity, and fruitfulness. In the West the* boteh *motif is usually described as a 'paisley' design.*

146

It has been said that the Indian subcontinent is the most original, creative and prolific source of patterned textile production in the world. Certainly the sheer beauty of the patterns, colours and textures produced in such exquisite profusion by the many skilled weavers, dyers and embroiderers is breathtaking. In the past a girl would spend all her youth stitching and embroidering garments and accoutrements for her dowry. Today, rural life has changed irrevocably and there is no longer the time or need. The beautiful hangings for sale today are often from the dowries of women who married 30 or 40 years ago. Today, rural villagers embroider for the tourist market or export rather than for their own use. Though commercialised, the products still retain much of their traditional charm and originality.

*South Asia*
# India & Pakistan 2

147

148

149

150

**147** *Bodice detail from a modern Baluchi woman's dress, from near the Afghan border. It is worked in hand-sewn chain stitch with appliqué gilt thread and decorative punched brass buttons. The symmetrical arrangement of squares within a square is characteristic of embroideries from this area.*

**148** *A pattern made up from lotus motifs – symbolic of the sun – is set into a simple diamond grid. The vitality of the design springs from the way that near-identical motifs vary in form. This detail comes from a modern child's dress from northwest Pakistan.*

**149** *While at first glance this pattern looks like a good example of a basic folk design, its simplicity demonstrates a deep understanding of how colours relate to one another. The detail is from a bedding cover, from Patel in northwest Pakistan.*

**150** *A section from the bodice of a modern woman's dress, from Sindh in Baluchistan. The mix of pale colours and the use of circles set symmetrically within a framed border is characteristic of embroideries from this area.*

**151** *From Kutch, northwest India, this modern fabric comes from a young married mother's blouse. The parakeets, the flowers and the colours are all symbols of bounteous plenty – vital in a blouse worn by a mother with a child at her breast.*

South Asia
# India &
# Pakistan 3

**152** *This dynamic pattern forms part of a woman's blouse from Pakistan. It is embroidered in silk using a stitch that radiates out from the centre of the motifs. The use of small square motifs set within a border, with selected squares being turned so that they are aligned on a diagonal axis, is characteristic.*

**153** *A piece of embroidery from a knuckle shield, made in Rajasthan. The use of the victorious lion motif suggests that it belonged to a warrior for whom the motifs of conquest would have been a talisman.*

**154** *A section from a cotton shawl made in the Swat valley area in the mid-19th century. It is interesting to note how the motifs within the large squares – the octagonal shapes – look very much like the Persian gul, or rose. This motif is the base decoration of almost all Turkestan carpets.*

**155** *Although this is a modern piece, the colours, forms and spiralling pattern on this man's wedding scarf suggest it draws inspiration from much earlier embroideries. It is probable that*

152

153

designs such as this were passed down through the family. This example was made in Sindh in Pakistan.

**156** Part of a wall hanging made in Gujarat in the 1950s. All the motifs have been appliquéd – that is, cut from scraps of fabric and sewn on to a base cloth. Interestingly, some of the scraps used to make the figures have been cut from much older pieces of cloth. American and European folk artists created their patchwork quilts in much the same way.

**157** From Gujarat, this 19th-century silk embroidery on a woven silk base is a rare example of a hanging for a temple dedicated to Vishnu the Pervader or Sustainer – literally from the Sanskrit, 'the god who works everywhere'. The scenes show episodes from the life of Krishna and the incarnate form of the Hindu god. The primary detail – the god within the pavilion, complete with cushions and handmaidens – is a widely used motif on paintings, illustrations and fabrics.

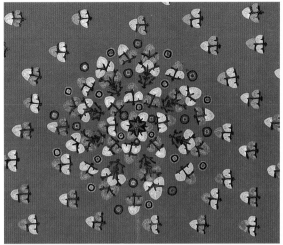

155

156

154

157

*South Asia*
# India &
# Pakistan

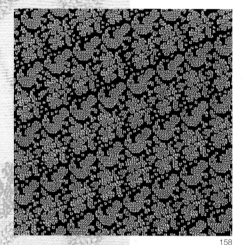

158

160

159

**158** *Embroidered in silk thread
on a woven silk ground cloth, this
design features the* boteh *motif –
a stylised fig or pinecone – and a
small bird and flowers. This early
20th-century piece was obviously a
valued item since its workmanship
is of the very highest quality.*

**159** *A detail from a late 19th-
century cloth cover, in embroidered
silk on a woven cotton ground.
The small flower symbols are
possibly stylised roses – a symbol of
well-being.*

**160** *The motif repeated on this cloth takes its shape from the lotus flower, a symbol of happiness and fertility. Made in the early 20th century, it is embroidered in silk, with silver thread and beads, on a woven silk ground.*

**161** *A detail from a ritual cloth, made in Assam in the 17th century. The fabric is silk lampas (ornate cloth similar to damask) weave on a plain silk ground. The pattern features Assamese inscriptions and scenes from the life of Vishnu with related symbols, such as the wheel of life.*

**162** *The shape and structure of the stylised flower motifs, and the way they are arranged on the ground, suggest that this late 18th-century shawl was made specifically for the European market. The pattern is embroidered in silk on a plain woven cotton ground.*

**163** *A detail from a late 19th-century marriage canopy, comprising embroidery on a cotton ground. The motifs on the design are good luck symbols – all the gods and deities needed to ensure a smooth-running household.*

**164** *The main motif seen in this detail – a* boteh *– is made up of a group of flowers, very much in the style of carpet border designs as seen on some Afghan carpets. This early 19th-century bedding cover is embroidered in silk on a woven cotton ground.*

161

163

162

164

*South Asia*
# India & Pakistan 5

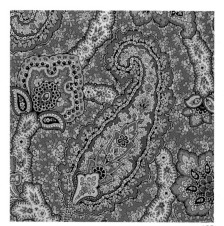

165

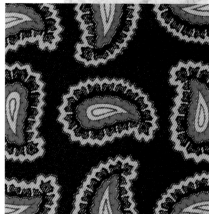

168

**165** *Part of a modern printed textile, featuring the* boteh *or* buta *motif commonly known in the West as a paisley pattern. Many Indian designers now claim that the* boteh *motif was stolen and misused by the West to such an extent that in the 19th century it brought about the collapse of the Kashmir shawl industry. Consequently, it is thought by many that the term 'paisley' ought to be used only for textiles made in England.*

**166** *A modern printed silk furnishing fabric, a French variation on the English paisley theme. While such fabrics bear little resemblance to the Indian originals, they have nevertheless been in fashion for nearly 200 years.*

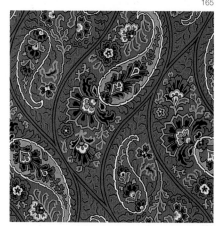

166

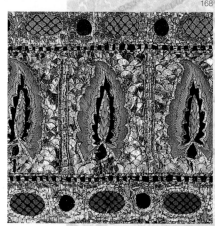

169

**167** *A typical English paisley design of the type usually associated with the woven silks used for ties. Such silky fabrics are known in the textile trade as* foulards. *This example is very different from the Indian originals – the colours are muted and the design is conservative.*

**168** *A standard modern Western paisley design, as seen on countless printed fabrics, from dressing gowns to ties. These designs, Indian in origin, have become classics in the West, perennially appearing in every kind of application.*

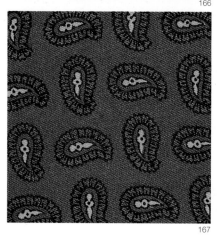

167

170

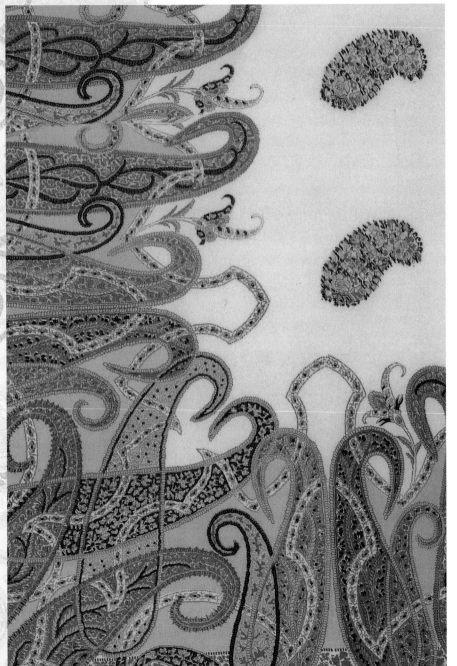

169

169 *A man's turban band, made in Lucknow in the first quarter of the 19th century – in a style that an official would have worn at court. The boteh motif is embroidered in silk on a woven cotton ground, with velvet appliqué, stitched sequins and embroidered silk-and-silver-thread additions.*

170 *Possibly a design for a European textile, this classic example of an original boteh motif was made in the early 19th century. It is painted in gouache on paper. The dense form of this boteh suggests that it has its origins in Kashmir, possibly as a motif from a shawl or kilim rug.*

171 *Fine woven wool with embroidered additions has been used to create this beautiful, high-quality shawl, produced in Kashmir in the early 19th century. Kashmir shawls can be divided into two types: those that are woven and those that are embroidered. Of the two, the woven shawls are considered superior since they are extremely time-consuming to make. A fine woven shawl can take up to 18 months to weave.*

171

*South Asia*
# India & Pakistan 6

**172** *A diaphanous dress fabric, woven and embroidered in Madras about 1855 as a piece of cloth made specifically for the European market. While cloths of this character are typically Indian in structure – they are beautifully hand-woven – it's also plain to see that the designs have been shaped to suit European taste, to the extent that they look more European than Indian.*

**173** *Wonderfully exuberant, this textile was hand-woven in Gujarat sometime in the middle of the 19th century. The stylised flowers are composed of woven strips of silver with couched metal strips, metal foil and pieces of beetle wing. The use of iridescent wing cases to embellish textiles is a practice that goes back to ancient times.*

**174** *Made in Gujarat in the 18th century specifically for the European market, this length of fabric takes its design inspiration from English Jacobean embroidery.*

172

173

174

175

176

The most likely scenario is that the European trader would have given the Indian producers a pattern to follow. The fabric is embroidered in silk on a woven cotton ground.

**175** The swirling leaf motifs on this delicate dress fabric are composed of couched gold, wrapped thread and twisted gold wire, with sequin and beetle-wing additions. The motifs are embroidered on to a woven cotton net base, but for preservation and display reasons the net has since been mounted on a base of stout cotton cloth. This fabric was made in Hyderabad in the middle of the 19th century.

**176** Woven in cotton and embroidered in silk, this length of dress or furnishing fabric was made in Gujarat in the late 18th century. It takes its inspiration from the French 'bizarre' patterns that were fashionable at that time. The pattern is made up from a mishmash of Indian and European images and motifs.

*South Asia*
# India &
# Pakistan 7

177

178

**177–178** *Of fine silk embroidery on a woven cotton ground, these two lengths of dress fabric were made in Gujarat in the 18th century for export to England. The un-Indian look of the designs suggests that the trader supplied the Indian weaver with a piece of English embroidery to copy. The design on the left (177) is a faithful copy of English crewelwork.*

**179** *An appliqué cotton coverlet, with cotton running-stitch embroidery, made in Gujarat in the last quarter of the 20th century. The elephant motifs – symbols of wealth and prosperity – are a typical choice for an infant's cover.*

**180** *English flowers, Indian turbans and swags and Hindi script are here all thrown into an exuberant, if slightly curious, mix. This machine-printed fabric was made in Manchester, England during the 19th century, for export to India.*

**181** *The decoration is unmistakably Indian, but this 19th-century cloth was machine-printed in England. By this time there had been a complete turnabout: woven English cloth was being printed with Indian motifs in England – sometimes by Indian manufacturers – and exported to India.*

**182** *Appliqué details are combined with silk embroidery in this 20th-century woman's shift, produced by members of the Hindu community in the Sindh area. The zigzag design with its infill of dots is typical of the region. Shifts of this type are still made and worn.*

179

181

180

182

*South Asia*

# India & Pakistan 8

**183–184** *While the flower motifs of these designs are different, both patterns spring from the diamond grid, known all over India and across Persia as the* mina-khani *or 'beautiful garden' design. The illustrations show details from Indian textiles, widely seen in the Great London Exhibitions of 1851 and 1855 and later published in 1856 in Owen Jones's influential book* The Grammar of Ornament.

**185** *The primary motifs shown here are variations on the characteristic* boteh *motif, known also as the almond or Kashmir design, one of the most widely used motifs in Indian textiles.*

**186–188** *The naivety and directness of these patterns shows how it is possible, with no more than two blocks and two colours, to build really dynamic patterns. The birds and flowers are symbols of fertility, prosperity and happiness – seen on everything from textiles to jewellery and woodcarving. The grouping of the flowers on the diamond is known in Persian as* mina-khani: mina *being a woman's name and* khani *meaning house or garden. The idea is that if a man has a wife, a happy house and a beautiful garden, then he has paradise.*

**189** *The open-hand motif utilised on this cotton fabric symbolises giving, receiving, and blessing. The hands are dotted and while it is possible that this refers to the stigmata on Christ's palms (many of these prints were bound for export), it is more likely, given the provenance of the fabric, that they reproduce the lucky dot of henna widely used by Hindus.*

183

184

185

186

187

188

189

190

191

192

**190** *A detail from a cotton fabric printed in four colours – black, orange, yellow and green – using four wooden blocks. While many of the motifs are simply depictions of flowers and foliage, the orange rosettes symbolise the life-giving powers of the sun.*

**191–192** *The clematis-like climbing plants shown here symbolise beauty, well-being, longevity and tenacity – the hope being that the wearer lives a long, happy and fulfilled life. The design bears a striking similarity to those seen on Turkoman carpets, particularly in the shape of the flowers and way the pattern is structured.*

**193** *While the motif used on this Indian textile – a vase with flowers – is common throughout India, many believe that its origins lie in Persia, where the motif is known as zil-I-soltan and is closely associated with royalty.*

193

194

195

# *Western Asia*
# **Persia**

194 *A reinterpretation of an 18th-century Persian embroidery. The stylised flower motifs are termed* khanch, *meaning house. The suggestion is that they resemble a field of flowers as seen around a noble house.*

195 *A detail from a 15th-century wall mosaic – a classic Islamic geometrical pattern based on hexagons – copied between 1869 and 1877 by Prisse d'Avennes, a traveller and compiler of some of the classic French pattern books.*

196 *A 19th-century artist's interpretation of an Islamic wall tile border. European artists of the period built motifs of this character into their designs on wallpapers, fabrics and tiles.*

197 *An illuminated 16th-century Persian manuscript. The twining complexity of the interleaved foliage recalls the figurative patterns of great classic pieces of Iznik porcelain.*

196

197

Rich surface decoration – whether of buildings, tiles or textiles – is one of the defining characteristics of Islamic style. And nowhere did the decorative arts flourish more strongly than in Persia (present-day Iran), especially during the Safavid era (1501–1722). Persian craftsmen from this 'golden age' were acknowledged as some of the finest in their field, and their work can be seen across the Islamic world. Many Persian rug and textile designs are based on flowers and elaborate 'arabesques' – a motif of intertwining vines, tendrils or branches. Tiling, by contrast, often adopts a geometric approach, set out with great precision using a grid and compass. These designs were eagerly adopted by European designers in the 19th century, usually based on pattern-book sources.

*Western Asia*
# Persia 2

199

200

198

**198–204** *These seven details all feature classic Islamic geometrical patterns, based on hexagons. The patterns are derived from 15th-century wall mosaics from Cairo, executed by a Persian artist. They were copied and painted by Prisse d'Avennes, the French collector and a great traveller, sometime between 1869 and 1877.*

*Although the patterns appear complex, if you take a close look at them you can see how they can all be achieved by using simple compass techniques. For example, the whole design for the stunning mosaic at far lower right (204) can be drawn using a technique today called the hex-step-off. It works like this: fix the compass (in early times, a cord with a sharp stick tied at either end) to any radius, draw out a circle, step off the radius around the circumference of the resultant circle, and then either draw straight lines to link alternate circumference intersections to make the classic hex star or draw straight lines to link neighbouring intersections to make hexagons.*

*Though these tile designs are technically no more than a mechanical play on compass-drawn geometrical forms, their creative complexity rises above simple geometry and elevates them to a much higher plane of aesthetics.*

201

202

203

204

*Western Asia*
# Persia 3

205

206

207

208

**205–206** *Persian pattern design has a long and distinguished history. These watercolour interpretations are from silk tapestry hangings dating from the 6th century. They feature the ancient Persian motifs the* senmurv *or winged dog, the winged horse and the royal lion. The designs have been compared with those created by Syrian or Egyptian weavers under combined Greek and Persian influence.*

**207** *A detail from a late 17th-century embroidered silk tomb cover. It is inscribed in Arabic with Qur'anic verses and the names of three figures. The motif in the centre is known as a* mahi, *a Persian word that means fish; it resembles the* herati *motif (stylised rosette) seen on many Persian carpets.*

**208** *The vase-of-flowers motif, known as zil-I-soltan, is typically Persian. This early 17th-century hanging is done in silk embroidery on a woven cotton ground.*

**209** *Flower tracery combined with peacocks is a popular Persian pattern, symbolising prosperity, well-being, good luck and immortality. The likelihood is that this design originally came from a marriage gift, probably a robe or hanging. This artist's interpretation was painted in the 19th century.*

## Western Asia
# Persia 4

**210–211** *Two illustration details from the border margins of a Persian prayer rug from the Safavid period (1501–1722), painted in the 19th century from museum examples. The stylised floral motifs, thought to be the rose and the fuchsia, are traditional interpretations of scenes of paradise. With paradise being likened to a fabulous garden – a place of calm and contentment, in some ways resembling the Victorian notion of heaven – the borders of the carpet were sometimes interpreted as high walls covered in flowers, like a walled garden.*

**212** *An English Victorian printed fabric design that takes its inspiration from a traditional Persian theme. The Victorians were captivated by all things Persian, to the extent that they copied these motifs – the rose and the peacock – from a museum exhibit rug and adapted them as furnishing-fabric motifs.*

210

211

213 *Broad, bold traditional Persian motifs such as this were taken by Victorian designers and adapted as 'exotic Eastern bazaar' tiles. This border design from a Persian carpet depicts one of the walls around the gardens of paradise.*

214 *This prayer rug draws its inspiration from the Safavid rugs made in Persia during the second half of the 16th century. Apart from the inner border of stylised flowers, the entire pattern is made up of repeated inscriptions from the Qur'an, formed into an interlocking design.*

215 *A detail of a Persian prayer rug taken from a 19th-century European pattern book. While the mix of motifs suggests that the illustrator felt free to combine elements from a number of different rugs, the interlaced pattern of floral motifs looks very much like that found on the famous Ardebil carpet in the Victoria & Albert Museum in London.*

212

214

213

215

*Western Asia*
# **Persia** 5

**216** *This fan-like motif is a stylised interpretation of the peacock's tail – a symbol of long life and nobility. This detail comes from a woven textile, possibly 17th-century.*

**217** *A detail from a woven textile, possibly 19th-century. The pattern forms are much the same as those seen on Turkoman carpets, with Kizyl-Ayak-type gul motifs placed on a diamond grid, with stylised flowers all around.*

**218** *A complex geometrical serriform pattern makes up this 14th-century wall mosaic, reproduced by a Victorian artist. If you look closely at the main part of the design you will see that the red-brown part of the pattern is created from a single tile form, while the cream and black patterns are made up of three forms. The tilemaker had only to make four different tile shapes for the whole design.*

**219** *Persian design is especially renowned for its rich array of floral motifs. This illustration shows a 16th-century ceramic*

*wall detail from the mosque of Ibrahym Agha. The tracery of stylised flowers, set on to a diamond-gridded ground, resembles patterns seen on Persian floral niched prayer rugs and embroideries. Here, however, the design has been simplified so that it can be broken down into a number of repeat tiles.*

218

221

216

219

222

217

220

223

224

**220** *Detail taken from a 14th-century ceramic wall pattern. Many of these wall friezes took the form of glazed bricks. The design was divided up into repeat sections, each section was subdivided into so many bricks, and then the outward face of the brick was dipped in the appropriate glaze and fired.*

**221** *This intricate geometric design employs the traditional Islamic theme of interlaced equilateral triangles set alongside and within hexagons. The detail comes from a wall mosaic from a 12th-century mosque, painted by a 19th-century illustrator.*

**222** *A Victorian pattern-book illustration showing a 17th-century ceramic wall detail from the mosque of Beyt el-Emyr. Motifs such as this were adapted for fabrics and wallpapers in the 19th century.*

**223–224** *Details from two 14th-century silk wall textiles using the characteristic peacock motif. In early Christian symbolism and in Islamic tradition, the peacock represents immortality (its body was thought not to decay), paradise (because of its exotic beauty) and spiritual rebirth (from the way it spread its wings, and the belief that it dwelt in paradise). While the mirror imaging of the motifs is a design ploy to create a dynamic quality, it is also a function suited to and made easy by the weaving process.*

## Western Asia
# Persia 6

**225** *This lozenge-shaped pattern can be found on the walls of the Alhambra – a citadel and palace in Granada built for the Moorish kings during the 13th and 14th centuries. This particular detail comes from a wall panel from the Hall of the Abencerrages. Note the characteristic stylised pineapple motif at the centre.*

**226** *Another example from the Alhambra showing a section from the panelling on the walls in the Tower of the Captive. The interesting thing about this pattern is the excitement it stirred up when it was first seen. It led Herbert Minton to design a whole range of tiles and mosaics now present in countless 19th-century villas, churches and public buildings.*

**227** *A drawing from Owen Jones's* The Grammar of Ornament *showing a detail from the panelling of the Hall of the Ambassadors in the Alhambra Palace. While the palace has now been restored, when Jones made his original drawings, the whole complex was in semi-ruin: sheep and goats roamed freely and early tourists collected fragments of loose ornament as souvenirs.*

225

228

226

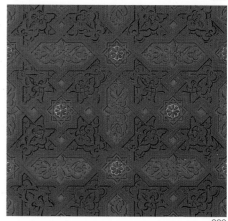
229

227

230

231

232

**228** *Another design from the Alhambra. Immediately after seeing it, Herbert Minton commissioned designers to reinterpret it in the form of a tiled panel.*

**229** *Owen Jones described this particular design as 'the great arabesque'. Although based on a circle, the repeats create octagonal shapes, whereas most Western circle-based designs are hexamerous forms – that is, repeated together, they create hexagons, hex-stars, and other six-sided forms.*

**230** *The interlaced pattern here always relates to an even underlying grid made up of a mix of horizontal, vertical and diagonal lines.*

**231** *A detail from the ceiling of the Portico of the Court of the Fishpond at the Alhambra. Note the artist's complete mastery of geometry, the design being based on the relationship between the square and circle.*

**232** *Another design based on the geometrical interplay between the horizontal axis and the hexamerous angle of 60 degrees.*

233

234

235

236

**233** *Stylised pomegranate trees are placed within ogival medallions in this late 16th-century fabric from Turkey. The pomegranate tree is an Eastern symbol of plenty.*

**234** *The motifs running vertically in these bands are stylised patterns that symbolise the Tree of Life. This detail is from a 19th-century prayer rug from Turkmenistan, made by the Yomud nomads.*

**235** *A border detail from a 19th-century Shiraz carpet. The border details of carpets of this type are characterised by geometric motifs executed in straight lines that run at a diagonal angle to the carpet's selvedge or guard border.*

**236** *A herati motif painted by a European artist in the 19th century. The herati motif is composed of a central rosette enclosed in a diamond. Experts can identify a carpet – when, where and how it was made – simply by the shape and structure of the herati motifs.*

## Central and Western Asia
# Caspian Region

East meets West in this vast region, which stretches from the Bosphorus to the Chinese border. Across the steppes of Central Asia ran the ancient Silk Road, whereby Chinese fabrics, porcelain and other goods travelled far afield. Motifs such as the 'cloud band' and 'dragon' entered the Near Eastern design repertoire via this route. Further west, the land of Anatolia, today the Asiatic part of Turkey, has long been famous for its weaving; some of the earliest known pile carpets originated here. The hardy, nomadic peoples of Central Asia left their own distinctive pattern-making legacy. Their brightly coloured rugs, covers and containers were an essential part of their everyday lives, and tribal symbols – such as the octagonal *gul* and the *herati* stylised rosette – were passed down generations with few changes.

*Central and Western Asia*

# Caspian Region 2

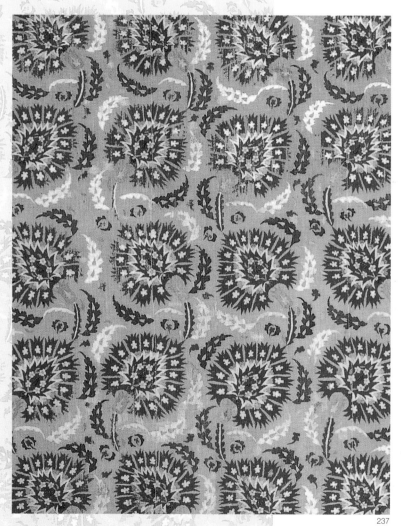

237

238

**237** The recurrent Eastern symbol of plenty, the pomegranate tree is here arranged as a stylised motif flanked with leaves. It is embroidered in silk on a plain woven ground. This facing for a quilt or hanging was made in Turkey in the mid-18th century.

**238** The layout of motifs on this 19th-century Turkish saddlecloth or fireplace overmantel panel suggests that it draws its inspiration from a much older Turkoman rug. The piece is embroidered in gilt and silk thread on a woven silk ground.

**239** *A hanging or quilt cover made in Turkey in the 17th century. This motif is also a stylised pomegranate, but it is interesting to note that while it shows a symmetrical interpretation of a pomegranate tree, the total motif also shows a cross section through the fruit.*

**240** *A border detail from an early 19th-century Turkish bath wrap — like a huge towel — with rose and tulip motifs set on a diamond grid.*

**241** *The maker of this sash has brought together three stylised forms — pomegranates, tulips, and hyacinths — to create a single hybridised plant motif. It is embroidered in silk and silver thread on a plain linen ground. The piece is thought to be Turkish, late 18th century.*

**242** *A section from a hanging or quilt cover made in Turkey during the last quarter of the 17th century. The stylised Tree of Life design has been created by setting the individual motifs on an ogival or point-ended tracery — a pattern structure that draws its inspiration from Turkish architectural forms.*

239

241

240

242

## Central and Western Asia
# Caspian Region 3

**243** *This highly decorated cover was made in Azerbaijan in the 18th century. The border around each of the star medallions features two characteristic motifs: the pothook (the pale hooked shapes that face each other) and the plant swastika.*

**244** *A typical Turkoman diamond motif – a detail from a rug – with a hook border. Note the earthy colours, characteristic of the region.*

244

243

245

**245** The typical eight-pointed star, as seen on many Turkoman carpets and rugs, can be seen clearly in this panel detail. The star is identical to some hex motifs on early American patchwork quilts and throws.

**246** An early 20th-century detail, illustrated by a European artist, from a Turkoman rug. The pattern features the characteristic ram's horn motifs, running 'Greek key' border and diagonal steps. The artist copied the detail with a view to reinterpreting it on a piece of German industrial pottery.

**247** A cushion cover from Daghestan. The design features a stylised sun with a swastika at its centre. The inner border running around the sun is made up of double-ended pothooks.
The pothook is a metal hook used by the nomadic weavers to hang cooking pots over the fire.

**248** This unusual Turkish textile is patterned with serrated diamonds and floral motifs. The design was included in a pattern book published in the late 1920s.

**249** A Turkish seat or cushion cover. The shape of the design suggests that it was inspired by a Turkoman original, but the lack of detail and the ill-defined character of the forms indicates that it was created by a copyist rather than a textile worker.

**250** The motifs in this silk hanging from Samarkand are blurred in the direction of the warp. This points to the fabric having been ikat-dyed. In this technique, both the warp and weft threads are bound and dyed before being woven.

246

247

249

248

250

*Central and Western Asia*
# Caspian Region 4

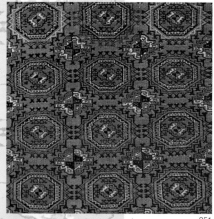

251

252

253

**251** *The stylised rosette or* herati *(the smaller hooked motif) and the larger stepped gul motif can clearly be seen in this detail of a rug from northern Afghanistan.*

**252** *The two white motifs on this wool rug detail are examples of the* harshang, *which in Persian means crab. The rug comes from the Bidzhov-Shirvan area. The shape and style of the central motifs suggest that this is a type of prayer rug known as a 'dragon'.*

**253** *A detail from a Khotan Samarkand carpet, made in Eastern or Chinese Turkestan. The arrangement of the hooked box motifs and the* harshang *or crab details, all set within a checkerboard grid, is characteristic of rugs from this area.*

**254** *A Bokhara or Tekke-Turkoman rug, made in Russian Turkestan. These rugs always feature gul motifs divided into four equal parts by lines that run the whole length and width of the carpet. The gul motifs, known as 'elephant's foot', are always arranged in lines so that they cover the entire central ground.*

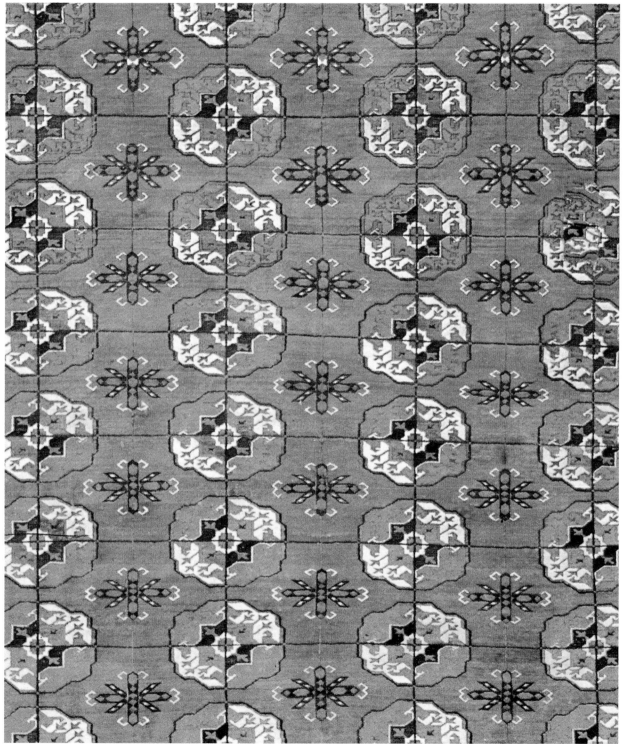

*Central and Western Asia*
# Caspian Region 5

**255** *A rich dark brown background throws the finely drawn pattern on this rug from Khotan into sharp relief. The design motif is the stylised flowering pomegranate tree.*

**256** *The central motifs on this rug – serrated leaves with hooks, and rectangles with hooks and checkerboards – are typical of rugs from the Caucasus region. This example is Kazak, made in the 19th century. At the edge of this detail you can see eight-pointed stars and small stylised animals, also characteristic features. The green, ochre and red colourway is also typical of the area.*

256

255

**257** *These large lozenges with the serrated edge and inward-pointing 'arrows' are a characteristic feature of Kazak rugs. They are known as the adler or eagle motif. In this 19th-century rug they are set out on a blue-black ground typical of pieces from this area.*

**258** *A Gendja rug woven in the Caucasus Mountains. This type of rug, with octagonal medallions on a dark ground, has a long history, borne out by the fact that they were depicted in European paintings – as tablecloths and wall hangings – as early as the 15th century.*

**259** *A Karabagh rug made in the Caucasus. The large pattern of massive serrated leaves with arm-like tendrils represents a stage in the development of the characteristic eagle or 'sword of Kazak' motif. At the centre, you will see a mix of stylised plant and animal forms.*

257

258

259

*Central and Western Asia*

# Caspian Region 6

260–262 *The Turkoman-inspired designs shown here became ubiquitous in the West during the late 19th and early 20th centuries. The designs were applied to everything from wall paintings, and wall and floor tiles, through to painted boxes and rugs. These examples are taken from lithographs drawn in 1879 in Bukhara (Bokhara) by the*

260

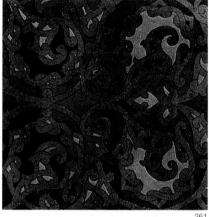

261

262

Russian artist Nikolai Simakoff for a pattern book published in 1882. Simakoff's interpretations are neatened versions of the originals. His copies are crisp and hard-edged with some motifs symmetrically reflected, while the actual items and artefact s are more lively and dynamic, with all the details demonstrating the objects' handmade quality and texture.

**263–267** When Nikolai Simakoff copied these designs from various items and interiors in and around Bukhara – wall paintings, tiled floors and carpets – he was overwhelmed by the variety of seemingly inexhaustible sources. The whole area was so rich in ornament that he realised that he could spend a lifetime and not begin to represent all the designs, patterns and motifs he saw. He wrote, 'The artist astonishes you by the facility with which he draws from the same designs dozens of new possibilities, without varying the colours at all. He is indefatigable in his work'.

263

265

264

266

267

*Central and Western Asia*

# Caspian Region 7

**268–269** *Two designs from woven silk ikat hangings that draw their inspiration from a whole range of sources including Turkoman carpets and nomadic Uzbek embroidery. The artistic representation of people and animals was, and still is, forbidden by orthodox Islamic belief. If you look within the designs, however, you will see that the women weavers who produced these motifs felt free to build stylised interpretations of human figures into their designs.*

269

268

**270** *The stylised motifs within this design – the hooked arm figures and the central gul or lozenge motif – point to this being a design from Yomut Turkoman women's weaving.*

**271** *A detail from an artist's interpretation, from a woven ikat, showing a stylised flower – either a pomegranate or a lily.*

**272–273** *The triangular motifs of these Turkoman bands, complete with dangling hooked appendages, are a* stylised representation of a Tamar, *a protective talisman worn to ward off the evil eye. Note also the small* boteh *motifs, like little teardrops, borrowed from Indian art.*

**274** *The shape of the central motif – the* gul *– suggests that this design is derived from a carpet woven by the Baluchi nomads of northeast Iran. While Simakoff describes this design as being from a Bukhara carpet, it is important* to note that 'Bukhara' carpets were (and are) not woven in that city, but in a huge tract of land that includes Turkmenistan and Uzbekistan.

**275** *A reinterpretation inspired by a woven ikat original. Although the nomadic weavers were roaming through Islamic lands where artistic representation of people and animals is prohibited, heavily stylised animal motifs may still be seen incorporated into their work.*

270

271

272

273

274

275

*Central and Western Asia*
# Caspian Region 8

**276–278** *A reworking of three designs, from Turkoman carpets, painted in 1879 by the Russian artist Nikolai Simakoff. It is possible to identify such carpets by the shape and colour of the motifs within the design. For example, in the design on the left, the octagonal shape of the gul motif, plus the infill of stylised branches, points to its being from an Afghan rug. In the central design, the lozenge shape of the gul with its fringe of hooks indicates that it is a Kazak rug from the Caucasus. As for the design on the right, while the lozenge shape of the guls suggest that it is a Turkoman rug from western or Russian Turkestan, it features so many mixed motifs that there is a strong likelihood that this design is a reinterpretation rather than a faithful copy.*

276

277

278

**279** *The eight-pointed star shape at the centre of the primary gul of this example, along with the latch-hook pattern that runs around the border medallions, is a strong indication that the pattern derives from a Shazhli (Shazhli-Shirvan) rug.*

**280** *The narrow banding of this design provides a clue to its origin. The work is a reinterpretation of Turkoman belt and harness strap design. When the designs were* published in 1882, they were immediately copied and reworked by countless artists, and reborn again – all over Europe – as patterns and motifs used in an immense range of applications.

**281** *The nomadic life of the Kurdish-Kazak women weavers is reflected in the way that the designs have always changed and evolved according to the movement of the nomads. Little by little, the* Kurdish-Kazak women absorbed designs and motifs from other tribes and other traditions.

**282** *A detail from Simakoff's pattern book that shows the corner from a Turkoman rug. A close inspection of the motifs that run around the border reveals scorpions and spiders, figures and the triangular Tamar or protective talisman – all stylised and reduced to simple easy-to-weave pattern forms.*

279

280

281

282

283

284

285

286

*Eastern Mediterranean*

# Classical World

283 *The various elements of this 19th-century sampler of Pompeian mosaic patterns demonstrates, through its eclectic shape and style of designs and motifs, how Roman artists drew inspiration from the art of conquered territories.*

284 *Illustration of an ancient Egyptian painted frieze. Note the concentration of rope, spiral and horn patterns, plus the animal-headed motif complete with horns and sun-disk crown. All suggest that the design was dedicated to the god Herishef.*

285 *With its discordant colours and abstract shapes this pattern looks very modern. It is in fact a pattern-book reinterpretation of an ancient Egyptian frieze. The zigzags and the lines springing from circles are typical ancient Egyptian motifs.*

286 *An illustration of an ancient Egyptian ceiling painting. The shape of the motifs suggests a Victorian reinterpretation rather than a faithful copy.*

The patterns of the ancient world exerted a longstanding influence: later generations reinterpreted the decorations on surviving artefacts again and again. Greek designs, with their geometric motifs and stylised plant forms, were largely disseminated through pottery. The vast extent of Rome's imperial territories ensured that its stonework and mosaic designs were widely known and, from the Renaissance onwards, artists flocked to Rome to examine the latest archaeological discoveries. This trend revealed unique painted friezes and frescoes, which sparked off a Neo-classical revival. At the end of the 18th century, Napoleon's campaigns in the Near East prompted a similar taste for Egyptian patterns and a further wave of Egyptomania, evident in many Art Deco designs, followed the discovery of Tutankhamen's tomb in 1922.

*Eastern Mediterranean*
# Classical
# World

287

288

289

**287** *A wealth of ancient Egyptian motifs is crammed into this mid-19th-century European illustration. Palms, chariot wheels and fan-like papyrus flowers are all rendered in vibrant colours. Such illustrations were adapted for multiple uses.*

**288** *This printed cotton fabric, produced in France in the last quarter of the 19th century, was no doubt inspired by Napoleon's successful campaigns in North Africa. This was a period when Europeans were fascinated by all things Egyptian. Note the cartoon cacti and the misunderstood shape of the pyramids.*

**289** *A detail from a watercolour illustration from an early 20th-century German pattern book, inspired by Egyptian originals. While the artist used ancient Egyptian imagery, from hieroglyphs and associated patterns, he reinterpreted them to suit the shape and composition of his own design.*

**290–292** *Three illustrations of Egyptian walls and ceilings from different tombs, painted in the 19th century for publication in a pattern book. While all three use imagery from nature – the date palm, papyrus and various flowers – the structure of the motifs suggests that they are actually drawn with a compass. For example, the foliage at the top of the palm is always drawn as three primary spiked elements with an arc over them, while the flowers are based on circles that have been quartered. It seems most likely that the European illustrator simply reinterpreted the designs in more contemporary form.*

290

292

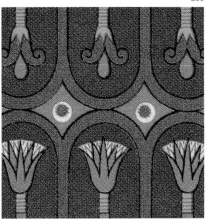

291

**293** *A mania for all things Egyptian swept through Europe and America following Howard Carter's discovery of Tutankhamen's tomb in 1922. This French silk chiffon scarf, with its rather fanciful interpretation of an Egyptian frieze, is typical of designs from that time.*

293

*Eastern Mediterranean*

# Classical
# World 3

294 *The stylised reinterpretation of a detail from a Greek vase shows pattern forms from the Greek Ionic order of decoration – the primitive zigzag at the top followed by egg-and-tongue ovolos, flutes and tongues – all typical of the Ionic period. The patterns are derived from naturalistic forms: the bud from Egyptian and Indian art and the repeated 'V' from Assyrian flower motifs.*

294

295

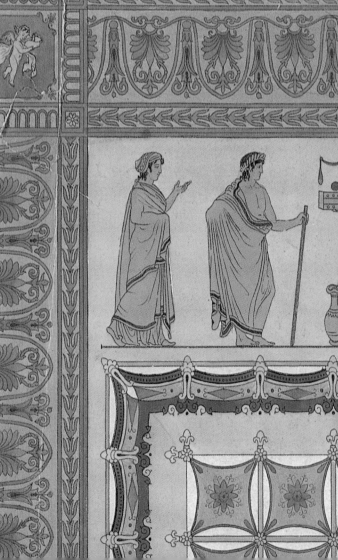

**295** The characteristic motifs shown here, derived from plant forms – possibly honeysuckle and vines – are achieved by stylising the details and drawing them so that the various forms are mirror images on a vertical axis.

**296** A detail from a French pattern book painted just before World War II. It shows a scene of a type found on Greek vases, albeit in a considerably elaborated form, while the border is more neo-classical than original in its intepretation.

**297** While the Greeks were close observers of nature, design dictates required that Greek artisans reduce the naturalistic form to a series of repeated motifs. It has been suggested that the characteristic shapes within these motifs have their beginnings in brush strokes.

**298** The running pattern – known by Turkoman rug weavers as a running dog and in the West as a Greek key – symbolises the everlasting circle of life.

297

296

298

*Eastern Mediterranean*
# Classical
# World 4

**299–301** *These impressions from the string course decoration on the Panathenaic friezes show two variations on the characteristic running swastika pattern. While such patterns are only seen as carved white marble today, it is now recognised that the carvings were once picked out in brilliant colours. To the ancient Greeks, the maze-like swastika represented good luck and well-being.*

299

300

301

302

303

**302** *This motif has been held to represent everything from flowers in a vase to an architectural fountain. It was widely used in fresco borders in the lost town of Pompeii and is usually seen composed using shades of ochre, brown and black.*

**303** *A reproduction of the cymatium of the raking cornice of the Parthenon. While experts argue about the roots of this characteristic motif, they all agree that the details from which it is made up are derived from the way a paint-loaded brush leaves a characteristic mark that is broad at one end and fine and tapered at the other.*

**304–307** *While all these patterns are clearly inspired by plant forms – vines, honeysuckle, laurel and ivy – it's also obvious that the forms have been reworked and stylised so that they represent plants in general rather than individual types. One element they all share is the way the stems, either as a straight line or as a wave-like curve, are embellished with secondary forms – dots, dashes and curls – that divide and fill the space to create a well-balanced whole.*

304

305

306

307

## Eastern Mediterranean
# Classical
# World 5

**311–313** *These paintings from Zahn's book* Pompeii *show combinations of stylised leaves, flowers and birds. The third painting in the sequence shows a pillar complete with a base, a central column and various dishes and basins with additional scrolls and details. Surviving pieces of Pompeian bronzework point to* this being an illustration of a piece of metalwork, possibly to sit in a courtyard. It has even been suggested that it is a form of garden ornament. The eye-level details – the way the viewer can see the underside of one of the upper dishes – suggests the artist was drawing an object much taller than the average person.*

**308** *A 19th-century impression of a 'scroll' frieze from the temple of Isis in Pompeii – published in a pattern book. While the author of the pattern book says, 'The artists of Pompeii invented as they drew; every touch of their brush had an intention which no copyist can seize', the fact that there are similar friezes in houses in Herculaneum suggests that the Pompeian artists were themselves working within a tradition with set conventions.*

**309–310** *This illustration by German artist Wilhelm Zahn (1800–1871) shows details of painted pilasters from the Forum of Hercules in Pompeii. Many of the painted designs are similar in form to those made in bronze. According to Zahn's famous book on Pompeii, published in 1828, the crisp character of various details that make up the motifs suggests that they were made using a mix of stencils and freehand brushwork. The likelihood is that the repeated details – the stylised leaves and scrolls – were created with the stencils, while the unique details such as the face were hand-painted.*

308

309

310

311

312

313

*Eastern Mediterranean*
# Classical
# World 6

314

315

**314–319** *Artist's illustrations showing six details from painted borders from various houses in Pompeii. The repetition of identical motifs suggests that these designs were achieved using stencils. The decorator would have prepared and painted the ground, drawn up a grid, established the position of a number of registration marks or guide lines within the grid, and then used a pierced wood or metal stencil plate and a brush to block in most of the broad forms. Finally, the master craftsman would have*

318

316

317

319

used a fine brush to sharpen up edges and profiles and to paint in individual images and motifs. The plant-inspired motifs all show a heavy Greek influence, and the patterns are composed of stylised motifs in flat tints, without any attempt to show roundness or form. But experts agree that the quality of the motifs – the actual way the forms are placed one to another on the walls of Pompeii – suggests the possibility that they were executed by painters who were more copyists than creative artists.

*Eastern Mediterranean*

# Classical
# World 7

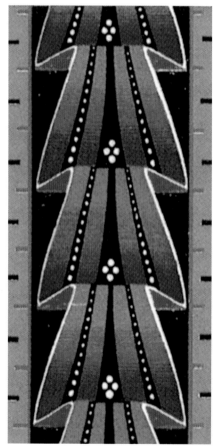

320

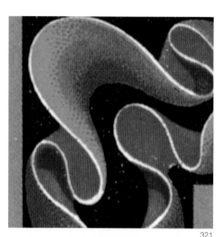

321

322

**320–321** *A 19th-century artist's reinterpretation of Byzantine patterns taken from an early manuscript. By the time the European artist had drawn the motifs to a different scale, substituted what he thought were suitable colours, and generally separated the motifs from their source, the patterns had become sketches rather than faithful reproductions. Despite this, when such designs were first published in Europe they inspired designers and manufacturers to think afresh.*

**322** *What's striking about this 19th-century design inspired by a Byzantine original is not its source, but rather the way the European artist has reinterpreted the forms by extending lines so that the total pattern has gained a solidity, depth and three-dimensional form uncharacteristic of true Byzantine work, which was usually rendered two-dimensionally, with a rather flat effect.*

**323** *The underlying grid of this particular 19th-century reinterpretation is derived from the Roman twisted rope motif, and the space between the twist and the border lines has been filled with stylised flowing foliage.*

**324** *The wide variety of motifs – Romanesque scrolls, stylised and mirror-imaged foliage, the Persian five-pointed leaf and the two forms of cross – perfectly express the mixed roots of Byzantine pattern. This example has been copied from the border of an ecclesiastic manuscript.*

**325** *With its running border and compass-worked roundels complete with the ribbon-worked swastika motifs, this design for a floor mosaic draws its inspiration from a whole range of Persian, Islamic, Greek and Roman sources.*

323

325

324

326

326 *Blocks of different colour and pattern are juxtaposed to make a dynamic pattern. This piece, woven in Ghana in the 1930s, is a typical example of a strip cloth – a textile made up from narrow strips of fabric that are sewn edge to edge.*

327 *Traditional African mud cloth is created by daubing a cloth with dye made from a mix of mud and leaves. This modern fabric, from Mali, has been machine-printed with a pattern resembling mud cloth.*

328 *A detail of a cotton cloth, made in Nupe, Nigeria. The pattern is made up of warp threads which have been so closely packed that the weft threads are hidden. The colours that you see are the warp threads.*

329 *Made in the 1950s by the Betsileo people in Nigeria, this woven silk cloth was used as a burial shawl or shroud. The cloth has been made up by sewing three strips together, side by side, along the selvedge edge.*

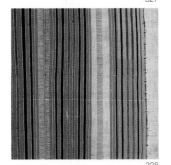

327

328

329

## *Africa*
# Sub-Saharan & North Africa

The strong craft tradition of sub-Saharan Africa has led to a rich array of styles and pattern-making techniques. Particular to West Africa are the distinctive 'strip cloths' made up from narrow pieces of woven fabric, often in highly complex arrangements. Elsewhere various tying, stitching and resist methods are used to pattern dyed fabric; the results can be highly colourful and vibrant. In Central Africa, raffia – the stripped leaves of a type of palm – is the traditional material, and Kuba cut-pile cloth is especially highly regarded. Away from the mainland, the island of Madagascar combines African traditions with southeast Asian and Arabian influences. Fabric printing is today an important export industry in Africa, with many designs adapted from the traditional craft techniques.

## Africa
# Sub-Saharan
# & North Africa 2

**330** *A modern cloth, roller-printed in Africa, that draws its inspiration from an old Nigerian strip-woven original. Fabrics of this character – machine-printed on a woven cotton ground – are made in Africa for export to the United States.*

**331–334** *Four details from cotton hammock cloths, woven by the Mende people in Sierra Leone between 1900 and 1934. While* the Mende weavers are well known for their warp-striped cloths, these examples are weft-faced – meaning these colours are created by having the tightly packed weft threads running or floating over a loosely packed warp. Selecting groups of warp threads creates pattern areas within the stripes – like the little band of counterchanged black and white squares.

330

331

332

**335** *While quilted patchwork cloths are not common in Africa, they were sometimes made for physical protection against arrows and spears. This detail comes from a horse armour quilt, made in Sudan at the end of the 19th century. The dots of tacking within the triangles have a structural purpose – they hold the layers of cloth together – but are also grouped for decorative effect.*

**336** *A high-quality cotton-and-silk strip cloth that was made by the Ewe people of Ghana sometime in the middle of the 19th century. This particular cloth was made by sewing alternate weft-faced and warp-faced strips side by side so that the nonalignment of the blocks of colour creates a slightly disturbing 'jumping' feeling of motion and vibrancy.*

**337** *Designed to imitate traditional woven strip cloths, this modern roller-printed cloth was produced in Africa for export. Printed cloths such as this are undoubtedly easier to make than the hand-sewn originals, but fail to achieve the same vibrancy. The regular stripes and somewhat muted colours show this is a mass-produced piece.*

333

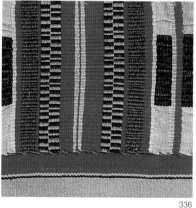

335

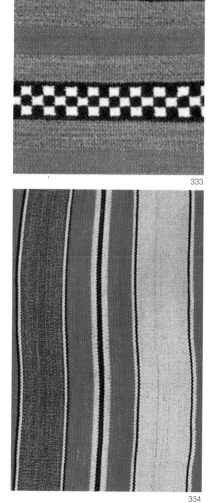

334

336

337

## Africa
# Sub-Saharan & North Africa 3

**338** *Section from a cotton cloth woven by the Mende people in Sierra Leone in 1934. The design is weft-faced. Selecting groups of warp threads creates patterns within the stripes – like the stylised motifs at the centre.*

**339** *Bands of different patterns and colours were arranged in a formal manner to make this woven cloth. This is a typical example from the Betsileo people of Madagascar.*

**340** *A man's cotton strip cloth woven in Ghana by the Ewe people in the middle of the 19th century. The weaving technique involves setting the loom up for a basic plain weave, and then introducing a secondary weft to create the stylised motifs.*

**341** *Ewe cloths are very carefully structured. The sections within the original narrow strips are woven in such a way as to form a basket-like pattern when sewn together to make the cloth. The stylised motifs are created by the introduction of an additional floating weft. This Ewe man's cloth was woven in Ghana in the first quarter of the 20th century.*

338

341

339

342

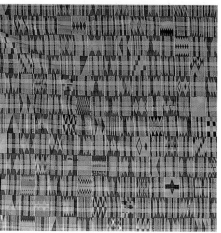

340

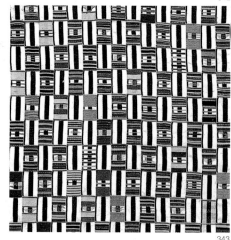

343

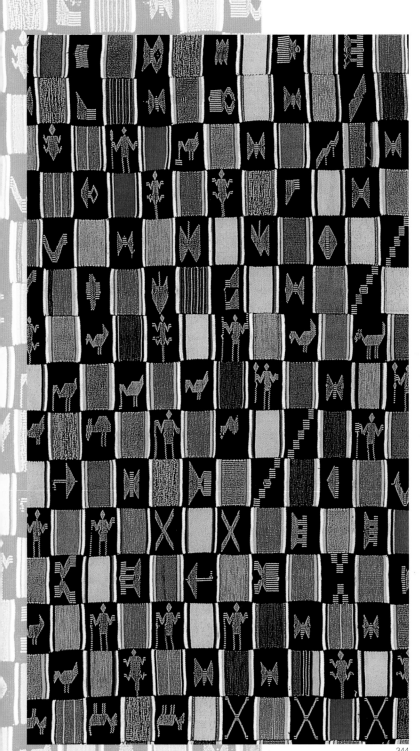

**342** *The name of this weave, an Ashanti design from Ghana, is 'my skill is exhausted', and it's plain to see why. Before weaving, the entire warp is covered with weft-float patterns set between weft-faced bands. The cloth is then woven in a continuous strip, cut into lengths and sewn edge to edge.*

**343** *Ewe-Adangbe man's cotton cloth woven in Ghana in the last half of the 20th century. While the composition of this cloth is both regular and carefully considered, the weavers view the orderly design as being of less value than their cloths with colour-band misalignments.*

**344** *A highly structured man's cloth by Ewe weavers. The excitement of the patterns within this cloth springs from the fact that the sequence of motifs within each stripe always varies, giving an element of unpredictability.*

**345** *The characteristic basket-like pattern of Ewe weavings can clearly be seen in this man's cloth. The overall design will have been meticulously planned and each fabric strip carefully placed. The juxtaposition of white with very dark brown provides bold contrast.*

344

345

*Africa*
# Sub-Saharan & North Africa 4

**346** *Despite the limited colour, the diamond pattern on this cloth has an interesting three-dimensional effect. This machine-woven fabric was made for the export market.*

**347** *This factory-woven cloth is an interpretation of a handmade Nigerian original. Commercial fabrics like these are made both for sale in Africa and export to the United States.*

**348** *The design of this Ashanti man's cloth differs from most West African strip cloths in that the different patterns are matched rather than misaligned. Cloths like this have been made since the early 18th century.*

**349** *A plain weave technique with supplementary weft inlay was used to create this traditional Ashanti man's cotton cloth. The dynamic pattern owes its success to the fact that the viewer must constantly try to make sense of the rhythm of white bars. The cloth was made in the mid-20th century.*

**350** *A modern African fabric that imitates much older Nigerian strip-woven cloths. Unlike traditional cloths made from woven narrow strips that have been sewn together, this piece is woven as a single broad width.*

**351** *Made for export, this modern cloth draws inspiration from traditional Nigerian strip cloths. Elements of traditional motifs have been adapted to fit factory methods.*

**352** *Stylised turtles feature on this modern factory-made interpretation of a traditional strip-woven cloth – possibly an Ashanti cloth from Ghana.*

**353** *A detail of a silk cloth made in Madagascar in the 20th century. The complex geometric pattern has been created by a technique that involves entering or floating bands of coloured weft threads over a plain warp. Cloths of this character are worn for special ceremonial occasions and are also used as burial shrouds.*

346

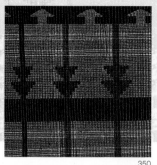
350

347

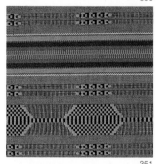
351

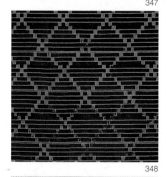
348

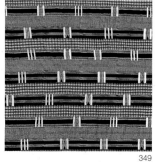
349

352

# Africa
# Sub-Saharan & North Africa 5

**354–355** *Two details from a cut-pile raffia cloth, made in Kuba, Zaire towards the end of the 20th century. The technique is much like velvet or rug weaving, in that the weft is heavily looped and then cut so that it becomes a smooth pile.*

**356** *A combination of resist and tie-dye techniques was used to create the pattern on this raffia cloth from Zaire. Some areas were painted with a thick starch paste, others were stitched and tightly bound, and then the whole piece was dropped into a dye vat. The paste and bindings were later removed to reveal the final pattern.*

**357** *A beautiful and characteristic adire, or resist-dyed cloth, made by the Yoruba people in Nigeria sometime in the middle of the 20th century. The ground was divided up into a grid, the grid was blocked in with painted freehand motifs – in a thick starch paste – and then the cloth was dipped in a vat of indigo dye. This pattern involved at least two separate dippings.*

**358** *Colourful stripes, chevrons, and a flower motif are combined in this detail from an Ethiopian tunic. This type of garment was worn by noblewomen in the 19th century. Chinese silk thread was used to embroider on to a base of machine-woven calico, which was imported to Ethiopia from Manchester, England.*

**359** *A large piece of cloth made by the Ashanti in Ghana in the early 1950s in a style that was thought to give protection to the wearer. Such cloths were made by at least two people, probably men, one to draw out the basic grid and fill in the magical Islamic designs and motifs, and one to draw in the Qur'anic inscriptions.*

354

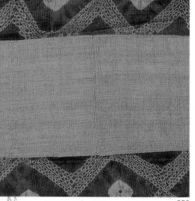

356

355

357

358

*Africa*
# Sub-Saharan & North Africa 6

**360** *This large woollen tent cloth was woven by Berber women in Morocco using a simple horizontal loom. The pattern is achieved by carefully selecting and lifting individual warp threads, and by laying short lengths of coloured weft in place.*

**361** *A detail of a cotton cloth woven in narrow strips by the Mende people in Sierra Leone in the early 1930s. If you look at the pattern closely you will see that the edge-to-edge joins occur in the wide, dark brown and cream and light brown and cream passage – hidden away between the cream and the light brown. In action, the weaver weaves a single long strip – as long as the loom will take – and cuts this up to make the cloth.*

**362** *The royal colours of blue and green have been used to create the stripes of this silk textile, woven by Merina people in Madagascar sometime towards the end of the 19th century. With its distinctive weft float pattern, this piece is evidently a special cloth intended for a wearer of high rank.*

360

361

**363** *The intriguing collection of images embroidered on this silk cloth suggest that it was made for a tribal chief. The nine linked squares guard against the evil eye, while the crossed circle used in conjunction with the spiral are motifs designed specifically to protect a chief. The cloth was woven by the Nupe tribe in Nigeria towards the end of the 19th century.*

**364** *A section from a cotton-and-rayon strip cloth woven by the Yoruba in Nigeria in the late 1930s. The cloth is 10 feet (3 metres) long and is made up of about 20 narrow strips sewn edge to edge, so it would have required about 200 feet (61 metres) of strip cloth to make up the total design.*

363

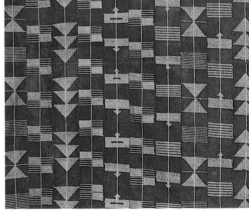

364

362

*Africa*
# Sub-Saharan & North Africa 7

365–366 *Timeless in their simplicity, these two cotton prints are influenced by traditional Mali mud-cloth work. This technique involves painting a mud-based dye on to cloth to create characteristic white or cream patterns on a black or brown ground. These modern cloths were factory-made for export to the United States and Europe.*

366

365

**367–368** *The designer of these modern roller-printed, factory-made fabrics obviously wanted to give them a generalised African feel rather than imitate a particular technique. A range of references, including Kente strip cloths and Malian mud cloths, have been put into the pattern mix. The burnt orange and black-brown hues add to the overall effect. Described by the makers as 'African tribal', these textiles are not for the pattern purist. The rest of us, however, can enjoy their energetic, free design.*

**369–370** *Two modern printed cloths, factory-made in Africa in imitation of Mali mud cloths. If these two designs look slightly familiar – a little like some of the textiles that were being made in America and Europe in the early 1970s – it's not surprising. Many of the designers of the period happily borrowed from ethnic art in general and the patterns of Mali mud cloths in particular.*

367

368

369

370

*Africa*
# Sub-Saharan & North Africa 8

**371–373** *Details of three modern African roller-printed designs. While the designers of these examples wanted to achieve patterns that were unmistakably African, they also wanted the designs to appeal both to Africans and to non-Africans. Therefore they didn't feel the need to relate to any single tradition. With the focus of the design resting on pattern and colour, they were content to bring together a whole range of images and motifs, regardless of their tribal origin, technique or material. And they weren't worried about bringing in designs from other periods. For example, the design on the far left (371) refers both to the African tribal tradition and to the so-called 'primitive' designs that became popular in Europe during the early 1950s.*

371

372

373

**374** *Bright, sunny and bold, this modern African design has been inspired by the imagery of traditional tie-dye. The technique involves bunching material, tying it securely and then dipping it into a dye vat. This results in bursting flower-like patterns – echoed in this factory-produced print.*

**375–376** *Two modern African commercially produced fabrics. If you look closely at the designs you will see that they look very much like the stylised patterns that you see on African relief woodcarvings – a number of zigzag patterns linked by small squares and triangles. In the context of woodcarving, designs of this character are achieved by using a small knife to repeatedly make six cuts that result in the characteristic triangular pocket.*

374

375

376

377

**377** *A detail from a fragment of woven textile found in Peru. Although first identified as 15th-century, it may be older. The design features the characteristic 'wave'-shaped pattern and a repeat motif of a cat-like animal – similar to motifs found on pottery of the Nazca period (c. 200 BCE–500 CE). The mummies of the dead were often wrapped in such cloths.*

378

**378–380** *Three textile fragments found in the tombs at Ancona, an area on the southwest coast of Peru, and made sometime about 400 BCE. The zigzag pattern is a characteristic feature of the so-called Paracas style, named after the Paracas Peninsula. While to some extent the pattern springs from the weaving technique – straight lines are easier than curves – the feeling is that the zigzags may well represent the lightning god, with the jags being symbolic of lightning. The bottom fragment (380) even shows the face of a rather terrifying-looking deity.*

379

380

A wide diversity of pattern-making traditions can be found among the indigenous peoples of the American continent, many of them stretching back to earlier cultures and civilisations. Some of the oldest surviving textiles come from tomb sites in Peru, providing us with a fascinating glimpse of South America's rich heritage. Designs created in present-day Mexico and Guatemala may well have their origins in the Mayan civilisation, which flourished in Central America about 300–900 CE. Mythical beings and symbolic motifs are found in patterns all across the American continent, testimony to the importance of the spiritual and the magical in many native cultures. Many apparently abstract designs, such as those of the Navajo, actually reflect myths and practices with a deep spiritual significance.

*America*

# Pre-Columbian America 2

381

**381** *A detail from a Navajo woven blanket, made in the traditional geometric style. It was woven in 1990 by Mae Curley. The zigzag lines represent lightning – a Navajo myth tells how the gods carry strings of lightning, which they use as ropes. The Navajo is the largest Indian tribe in the United States, occupying a large area of Arizona and New Mexico. They learned the craft of weaving from their neighbours, the Pueblo tribes.*

**382** *This Navajo blanket, made in 1940, is woven in the 'Tuba City Storm Pattern' style. The design draws its inspiration from the ancient Navajo art of dry-paintings or sand paintings, made by the shamans in their religious ceremonies. The pattern represents two figures performing a dance.*

**383** *The traditional Navajo 'gods' lightning' style, seen in* **381**, *is here given a modern interpretation. This detail comes from a blanket woven in 1970 in the Klagetoh area.*

382

383

384

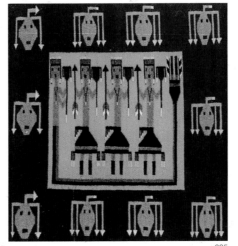

385

**384** *A detail from the centre of a modern Navajo round rug, woven by Lillie Hosteen about 1980. The motif represents a traditional dance. The Navajo began weaving rugs as a result of contact with Indian traders in the second half of the 19th century; prior to this they wove only blankets, for their own use.*

**385** *The design seen on this Navajo blanket, woven in the 1980s, is known as 'Storm Pattern'. It draws inspiration from sacred 'Yei' sand paintings, which feature a male divinity who is supposed to exercise great healing influence. In this detail the central figures wear skirts or loincloths complete with traditional tassels while the border comprises stylised head motifs.*

*America*
# Pre-Columbian America 3

**386–389** *Details from four Germantown Navajo blankets, made in the last quarter of the 19th century. 'Germantown' refers to the yarn used, some of which was made in Germantown, Philadelphia. The dazzling colours of the pieces are due to the synthetic dyes used in the manufacture of the yarn. Three of these blankets feature the characteristic Navajo zigzag and cross; these motifs have their origins in shamanistic sand paintings. The design at top right (387) is pictorial and therefore less typical. It is based on the stylised representation of a horse. Prior to the introduction of the 'Germantown' yarns, which were commercially produced, the Navajo used either wool from their own sheep or 'bayeta', a European-made woollen cloth that the weavers unravelled to make yarn.*

386

387

388

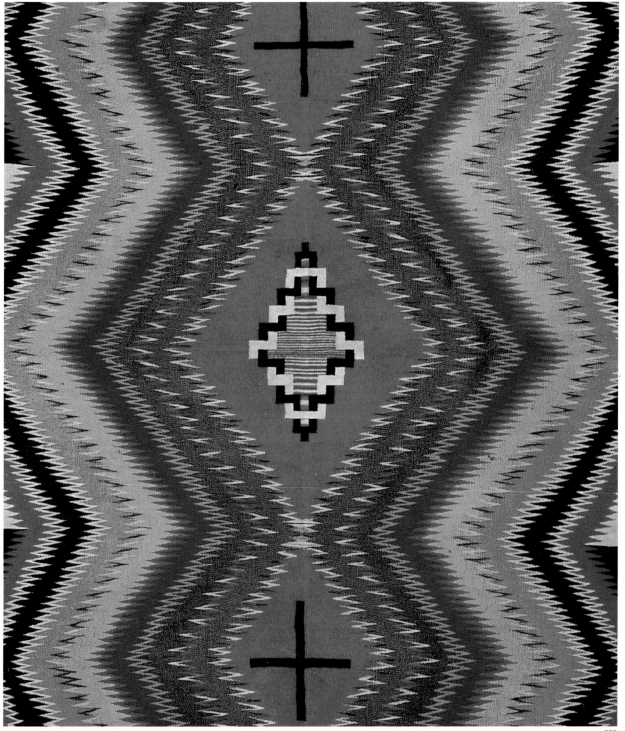

*America*
# Pre-Columbian America 4

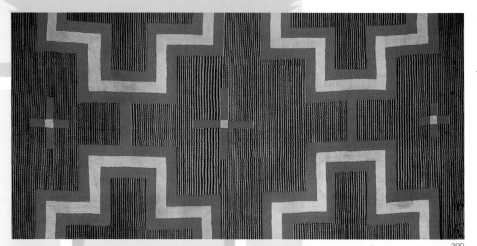

390

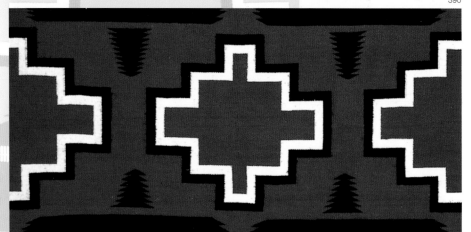

391

**390** *Boldly drawn stepped motifs dominate the design of this Navajo Germantown blanket. While the form of the pattern is to a certain extent shaped by the weaving technique – it is relatively easy to create motifs that square up to both the warp and the weft – experts also think that the stepped motifs had their origins in the terraced designs produced by Pueblo tribal potters.*

**391–392** *Two modern Navajo blankets, woven in what has come to be called the Hubbell Ganado style. In the late 1880s, the Indian trader John Lorenzo Hubbell together with partner C. N. Cotton opened a trading post at Ganado, Arizona. They and other traders encouraged production of weavings for 'Anglo' homes and went on to purchase all the blankets and rugs that the Navajo could produce. Around this time there was a move towards simplified and enlarged designs, very evident in the example at bottom left (**391**).*

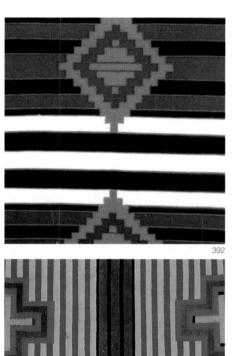

393 *Navajo patterns featuring the cross motif – seen here in a detail from a Germantown Navajo woman's blanket – are sometimes misguidedly described as being in the 'mission' style. In fact, the cross is a traditional Navajo symbol that predates contact with Christianity. Like other traditional 'wearing' blankets, this example, made about 1880, would have been worn around the shoulders.*

394 *A detail of a modern Navajo rug woven in Burntwood, Arizona, in what has come to be called the 'Burntwood' style. It is most strongly characterised by zigzags and stepped diamonds, and woven with commercial yarns that have been coloured with vegetable dyes.*

395 *Stripes and serrated diamonds combine to create a dynamic design in this Navajo blanket, woven in the so-called 'Moki' style. The blanket was made in the last quarter of the 19th century.*

392

393

394

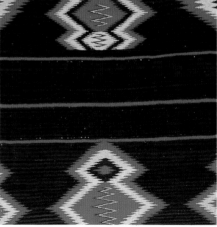

395

*America*
# Pre-Columbian America 5

396

397

398

399

**396–399** *Details from a selection of Chilkat blankets, woven at the end of the 19th century by the Tlingit tribe of the Pacific Northwest coast of North America. These blankets were worn by chiefs as ceremonial regalia. Extremely complex, they were created using a finger-weaving technique, rather than a loom, from a mixture of cedar bark and goat's wool. When, during the 18th century, European travellers first saw the work of the Northwest coast tribes – both weavings and woodcarvings – they were amazed by the vast range of animal motifs featured: ravens, thunderbirds, frogs, bears, beavers and wolves among them, many depicted full-face with wide eyes and arched brows. Just as the European coat of arms describes the status and background of the family to which it belongs, so these images show the status of the different clans and families and illustrate their relationships with the various beasts of myth and legend.*

400–402 *Mythical beings are*
*the subject of these three painted*
*woodcarvings, made at the end of*
*the 19th century by the tribes of*
*the Pacific Northwest coast. An*
*interesting feature they share is*
*the way in which the figures are*
*shown: just as in an architectural*
*drawing, the total design combines*
*a plan view, a front view, and two*
*side views, all wrapped up in the*
*same image. Within the image*
*all the parts of the animals are*
*depicted as stylised details. Eyes,*
*claws, teeth, mouths, beaks, and*
*feathers all appear in this flattened*
*graphic configuration. In this*
*society, every surface capable of*
*decoration – from the walls of the*
*houses through to sewn and woven*
*textiles – was ornamented with*
*totem figures and crests.*

400

401

402

406

*America*

# Pre-Columbian America 6

407

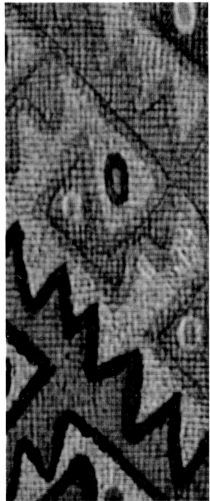

403

404

405

**403–404/406–408** *With their clearly defined patterns and intricate detail, these Peruvian woven textiles look fresh and vibrant. They are extremely old, probably dating to about 400* BCE*. They owe their excellent condition to the fact that they were buried in tombs, in hot and dry conditions. These examples come from the tombs of Ancona, on Peru's southwestern coast. They are woven in what has come to be called the Paracas-Nazca style, due to its similarity to patterns found on Nazca pottery and burial weavings from the Paracas Peninsula. Weavings such as this were often wrapped around mummies to form bundles, sometimes containing several hundred textiles. Some of the designs are fairly simple and geometric; others, such as pattern* **406**, *incorporate curved motifs, which would have been very complex to weave and would have been buried with a high-ranking person. The motif in pattern* **407** *shows a warrior complete with regalia and a feathered headdress.*

**405** *A detail from a Pueblo tribal pot, made by the Zuni tribe in the second half of the 19th century. The stylised deer and curved shapes seem at first glance to have some similarities to Celtic design, but the cream-and-brown palette is more characteristic of Indian work.*

**409** *This strikingly graphic and modern-looking design comes from a Tiahuanaco tapestry, found in the southern highlands of Peru near Lake Titicaca. The Tiahuanaco culture rose to prominence in Peru about the 7th century* CE. *Tapestry such as this was generally reserved for weavings of the highest status.*

408

409

*America*
# Pre-Columbian America 7

**410** *A detail from the neck of a Mexican man's shirt, embroidered in cotton on a plain weave ground. Although made in the last quarter of the 20th century, it draws its inspiration from much earlier woven designs. According to traditional Mexican beliefs all animals, and especially birds, have specific magical powers.*

**411** *The Guatemalan women who embroidered these motifs no doubt saw them as no more than traditional pictures passed down from mother to daughter. Evidence suggests, however, that their origins lie in ancient Mayan designs. They come from the collar of a two-panel* huipil, *a sleeveless blouse, made in the last quarter of the 20th century.*

**412** *A modern Guatemalan factory-made cloth, embroidered cotton on a plain weave ground. While many of these images are inspired by everyday life and are simply part of a design repertoire based on the flora and fauna of Guatemala, some of the motifs – for example, dogs, monkeys, turkeys and hens – depict creatures mentioned in the creation myths and retold in the Popol Vuh, the Mayan testament or holy book.*

**413** *Detail from the central panel of a Mexican bedspread – white cotton brocaded with coloured acrylic yarns – made on a backstrap loom by Ana Cecilia Cruz Alberto in 1977.*

*The design, with its wonderful display of animals, figures and buildings, was inspired by the brocaded* ayates *cloths or shawls, worn during local holy-day festivals.*

**414** *This traditional pattern, with its stylised tree and its various animals, all woven in horizontal bands and mirror-imaged, has its beginnings in pre-Conquest times when sacred trees were linked with the four points of the compass. The detail comes from a* quechquemitl, *a traditional cape made from two lengths of cloth, produced in the last quarter of the 20th century. The pattern is of cotton brocade on a plain woven ground.*

410

411

412

413

414

## America
# Pre-Columbian
# America 8

**415** *A detail from a woman's huipil or sleeveless blouse, made in Guatemala in the last quarter of the 20th century. The pattern is worked in a traditional weft-faced design. While some of the diamonds and zigzags are symbolic, for the most part the geometric designs have been used simply because the shapes – triangles, diamonds, lozenges and chevrons – lend themselves perfectly to the weaving technique.*

**416, 417** *A man's sarape, or cloak, woven in Guatemala in 1946. The central lozenge is in the form of a diamond, and similar shapes also make up the intricate pattern of the stripes, as seen in the close-up detail (417). The sarape takes the form of a blanket with a slot for the head. They were used by the Spaniards in South America as well as by tribes in South and Central America, who wear them to this day.*

415

416

**418** *This twisted figure of eight pattern is sometimes described as the 'twisted snake' motif. The likelihood is that it has its beginnings in the Mixtec people, from whom the present-day American tribes still using that name are descended. This detail comes from a woman's sleeveless blouse, made towards the end of the 20th century.*

**419** *A detail from an embroidered quechquemitl, an upper garment of cape-like form worn by Mexican Indian women. The two rectangular shapes on either side of the centre are derived from the four-headed eagle motif, which has been stylised to the point of abstraction.*

**420** *The 'blurred' effect on this pattern has been achieved by means of the ikat weaving technique, whereby the warp threads are tied and dyed before weaving. This detail comes from a silk rebozo – a woman's shawl – made in the last quarter of the 19th century in Santa Maria del Rio, Mexico.*

418

417

419

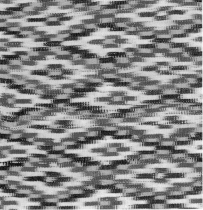

420

*America*
# Pre-Columbian
# America 9

421

**421** *The 'dead turkey' motif, seen here as a 'flattened' bird with downward-facing claws, is a feature of textiles made in three specific areas of Guatemala. It resembles the eagle found in ancient Mayan designs – unsurprising, given that two-thirds of the Guatemalan people are of pure Mayan descent. This detail comes from a* huipil *made in the last quarter of the 20th century.*

**422** *A detail from a young girl's huipil – a brocaded pattern on a woven ground – made in the last quarter of the 20th century in Guatemala. The design is made up of motifs that have been stylised to abstraction – for example, the eye that has become a diamond.*

**423** *This stylised bird comes from a fringed* tsute *– a square cloth used folded or draped on the head as a protective headdress, worn by both men and women – made in Guatemala some time at the end of the 20th century.*

**424** *The rabbit is thought to be a good luck symbol, symbolising fertility and general well being. Here it features on a late 20th-century tapestry-woven ribbon from Guatemala. Ribbons such as this are traditionally worn as hair bands and usually feature blocks of colour interspersed with animal motifs.*

422

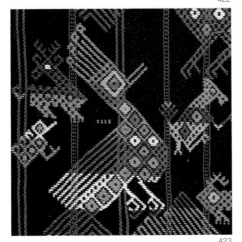

423

424

425

*America*

# Pre-Columbian America 10

**425** *Snakes – a symbol of lightning – and mythical double-headed condors make up the pattern on this woven and embroidered shroud. This ancient textile comes from the Paracas Peninsula in Peru.*

**426** *A detail from a Peruvian woven band. Long fabric bands of this character were – and sometimes still are – worn as belts and headbands. The zigzags are possibly symbolic of lightning, while the motif top right represents the eyes of a jaguar.*

**427** *A Peruvian textile fragment from the Paracas Peninsula. The stylised motif shows a warrior wearing a headdress returning from the hunt with trophies carried in his outstretched hands. This pattern is believed to be a very ancient one.*

**428** *Warrior figures hold a spear in one hand and a shrunken head in the other in this 14th-century Chimu-style textile from northern Peru. Collecting the heads of one's enemies was seen as a way of enriching physical and spiritual power in many tribal cultures.*

**429** *The falling figures in this textile depict dead ancestors passing from one spirit world to another. The detail comes from a blanket or cloak border, woven about 400 CE in the Paracas region of southern Peru.*

**430** *A stepped motif is combined with a geometric 'wave' in this old Peruvian textile. This particular design may have its origins in ancient basket-weaving techniques.*

426

427

**431** *A detail from a tapestry mantle woven by the Chimu-Inca Pachacamac culture – probably from the 13th century. The pattern is believed to show a warrior returning from a duck hunt.*

**432** *This Nazca-style textile was made about 500 CE in southern Peru. The two stylised counterchanged figures are thought to symbolise powerful opposites in nature: day and night, summer and winter, good and evil, male and female, life and death.*

428

429

430

431

432

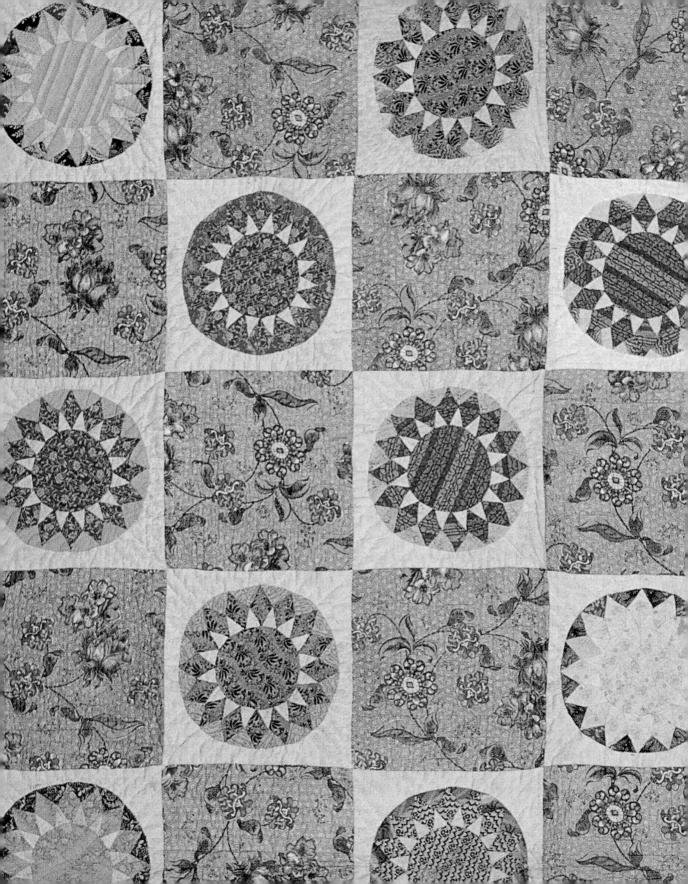

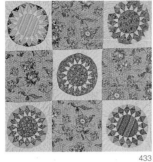

433

*433 A 'Sunflower' quilt, made in Connecticut in the mid-19th century by Mary Esther Hoyt Smith. The sunflower motif draws inspiration from the carved and painted decoration found on traditional hope chests. These chests were used to hold a young woman's accumulation of linen in anticipation of her marriage.*

*434 Nearly 4,000 patches were used to create this astonishingly intricate 'Sunburst' quilt. It was made in 1839 by Rebecca Scattergood Savery.*

*435 A detail from a quilt made in Riverton, Connecticut, in 1876 by 17-year-old Nellie Gates. Family history tells how this 'tumbling block' design used fabric patterns from her family's calico-printing operation.*

*436 A machine-printed patchwork design – an imitation – made about 1882 by a company called Cocheco. The design draws inspiration from much older patchworks.*

434

435

436

*America*

# Colonial North America

North America's strong quiltmaking tradition is reflected in this section: the patterns here are all either quilts or their printed imitations. For the early European settlers, patchwork quilts were a practical way of reusing valuable but worn fabrics. By the mid-19th century, however, North American quiltmaking had developed into an art form in its own right, with a distinctive pattern repertoire. Particularly notable are those produced by the Amish, a religious sect descended from European Anabaptists. Their bold, simple designs are characteristically plain as a result of strictly held religious convictions. Although these patterns were created after American independence, they are designated 'colonial' since they were created by the descendants of European settlers rather than by indigenous peoples.

*America*
# Colonial North America 2

**437** *A 'Diamond in Square' quilt made about 1925 by a member of the Lancaster County Amish. While the Amish needed to make quilts to keep warm, their strict religious rules governing social customs required that they stay away from 'showy' designs and patterns. Their quilts are pieced using only quite large areas of plain cloth, although the stitching patterns are sometimes very elaborate.*

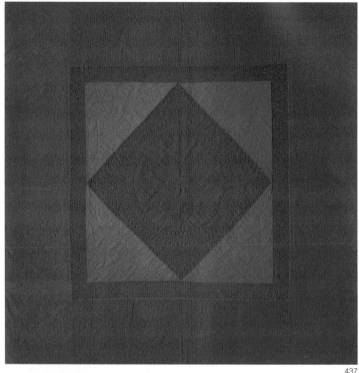

437

438

**438** *This Amish quilt is unusual on two counts. First, the 'Sawtooth Diamond' design is more complex than most Amish patterns, and second, we know the name of the maker. It was created in 1925 by Sarah Zook, a member of the Lancaster County Amish. The design draws inspiration from 18th-century German-Swiss* fraktur *motifs, as seen on Amish marriage and birth certificates.*

**439** *The bold, geometric design and startling colours make this quilt appear very contemporary. It was made in 1915 by a member of the Lancaster County Amish. The sophisticated mix of plum, cherry red and blue is entirely characteristic. In the past, many patterned non-Amish quilts were pieced only from scraps, but Amish work is frequently made from fabric purchased specially for the purpose.*

*America*
# Colonial North America 3

**440** *Detail from a quilt made in 1853 in New Milford, Connecticut, by Abby Jane Ferris Haviland and Arabella Ferris March. While many of the motifs are traditional pattern forms – German hex stars, English tulips, Swiss wreaths, and so on – the sequence of picture squares tells the story of the Ferris family, descendants of one of the founders of New Milford.*

**441** *The design of this quilt draws inspiration from the 'whirling sunflower' and tulip motifs seen in European woodcarving of the 17th century. The quilt was made in Pennsylvania in 1865.*

**442** *A quilt made in New Milford about 1830. The stylised acorn and oak-leaf motifs symbolise freedom, independence and longevity.*

440

441

442

**443** The similarity between the whirling sunflower motif seen on this quilt and the 'sun' symbol seen on Old World German hope chests suggests that the quiltmaker may have been of German origin. This vibrant marriage quilt was made in Pennsylvania in the last quarter of the 19th century.

**444** A detail from a marriage quilt made in Pennsylvania in the 1870s. The Pennsylvania German–speaking immigrants used the heart motif on a wide range of household items, from ironwork to pottery. The heart, signifying romantic love, was the most frequently chosen symbol for a marriage quilt.

**445** This 'Sunflower Fundraising' quilt was made between 1865 and 1890 by members of the Universalist Church of West Hartford, Connecticut. To raise money for church funds, church members each paid ten cents for the privilege of signing their worked patch. This style of quilt was quite frequently made by churches and benevolent societies.

443

444

445

446

*446 An illustrated detail
from the centre of the famous
Aberlemmo Cross from
Scotland, a monument or marker
formed from a single slab of stone
over 6 ½ feet (2 metres) high.
While the cross shape is of
Christian derivation, tradition
holds that the interlaced patterns
around the centre are Viking
motifs that were used as
protection against the devil,
misfortune, and the evil eye.*

*447–449 Illustrated details from
three other stone crosses found in
Scotland, all dating from about
550 CE. Little is known about
the precise origin of patterns
of this type. We do know,
however, that they are part of a
Scandinavian tradition that
spread southwards from Norway,
Sweden, Denmark, and Iceland
to England, Scotland, Ireland,
and beyond. The lower two
patterns (**448** and **449**) feature
the Celtic knot, or 'magic knot',
motif, made up of complex
interlaced ribboned forms that
lead seamlessly into one another.*

447

448

449

The Celts originated in central Europe during the Iron Age, but were gradually forced out of their homeland by the Romans and eventually settled on the western fringes of Europe. They were famous for their metalwork designs. These featured a range of versatile, abstract motifs woven together to create dense, hypnotic patterns. Occasionally, stylised animal heads and tails sprouted from the ribbon-like forms, adding to the richness of the mix. The Celts were pagan, but because there were so few figurative elements in their work, Christian artists found it easy to adapt their designs for use on sacred objects. Monks ornamenting their Gospel books borrowed freely from prehistoric Celtic patterns for borders and capitals. These lavish manuscripts were the showpieces of the early monasteries.

*Europe*
# Celtic 2

450–453 *Four examples from various manuscripts showing the Celtic knot style. The beautiful dragon-like image at top left (450) comes from the famous* Book of Kells, *dated to the first quarter of the 9th century. The image at top right (452) is from some Coronation Gospels of an unknown Anglo-Saxon king, while the two images at the bottom (451 and 453) are from the Sacramentarium of Rheims. There are various theories as to the meaning of the Celtic knot symbol. Some suggest that it has its root in an ancient pagan motif that was used to protect against the evil eye – the complexity of the design was so confusing that by the time an evildoer had worked his way around it, his evil powers were lost. The magic knot form is found in places as far apart as Ireland, Iceland, Germany and Russia, and in every kind of material, from wood and stone through iron, gold and silver, and in illuminated manuscripts.*

450

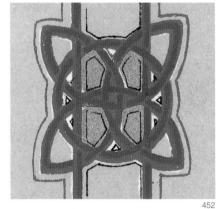

452

451

453

**454** *This initial letter features an infill of interlaced patterns and stylised animals. It is taken from the Lindisfarne Gospels, a beautiful illuminated manuscript produced in the Northumbrian island monastery of Lindisfarne at the end of the 7th century.*

**455–459** *Five illustrations from Owen Jones's 1856 pattern book* The Grammar of Ornament, *described only as 'examples of interlaced Celtic ornament – from various manuscripts'. These designs are invariably complex and some have features similar to patterns from locations as far afield as Russia and even China. The two bottom patterns (*456 *and* 459*) contain a swirling motif very similar to the Chinese 'yin–yang' symbol, while the repeat pattern of pattern* 455 *is not dissimilar to the traditional Chinese swastika. The Vikings were sea traders and evidence of their presence – and their design influence – has been found in England, Ireland, Greenland, North America and Russia. It was on the rivers of Russia, busy trading thoroughfares in ancient times, that they may have formed links with merchants from China.*

454

457

455

458

456

459

*Europe*
# Celtic 3

**460–463** *Four illustration details from various Irish sources showing a number of elaborate interlacing motifs, all more or less linked to the Celtic knot. These examples have been reworked from illuminated manuscripts, so they show rather smooth, polished examples of the characteristically complex patterns. An alternative theory to the one that maintains that the Celtic knot was thought to avert the evil eye is the idea that it was first invented as an illustration to an ancient folktale – from pre-Christian Scandinavian nomads – about two snakes that win a battle by consuming one another. The design far top right (**463**) closely resembles a* borre, *a type of knotted metalwork brooch favoured by 9th-century Vikings.*

460

461

463

**464** *A detail from a design that neatly illustrates the Scandinavian folk myth of the snake or dragon beasts devouring one another. Designs of this type – known as the 'Urnes' style, from the carved wooden decoration of a church in the town of Urnes in western Norway – represent the final, most delicate and most refined expression of Celtic ornament.*

464

462

465

**465** *The pattern of meandering leaves and stems that decorates this initial letter came to be known as the 'acanthus' style. This detail comes from a 12th-century illuminated manuscript.*

**466** *This detail, also copied from a 12th-century manuscript, offers a good demonstration of the way in which the Celtic knot evolved to become the early English acanthus pattern. As the acanthus style became more dominant, the Celtic stem disappeared.*

**467** *Portrait of St. Matthew from a manuscript illustrated in the 750s. The formalised draperies are a common pattern 'frame' for such portraits.*

**468** *A detail from a 14th-century Russian manuscript that harks back to what is known as the Viking 'Urnes' style, from the carved wooden decoration of a church in the town of Urnes, western Norway.*

466

467

468

The Church was the most important patron of the arts during the Middle Ages, so designers were called upon to decorate a huge variety of sacred objects. These ranged from lavish prayer books and stained-glass windows to liturgical vessels and vestments. The prevailing styles were Romanesque (9th to 12th century) and Gothic (mid-12th to early 15th century). The former was notable for its linear stylisations and the latter for pointed forms and a liberal use of foliate motifs. These found their greatest expression in the rose windows of the Gothic cathedrals, which constitute one of the glories of medieval art. Medieval designs enjoyed a new lease on life in the 19th century. The Gothic Revival, spearheaded by Augustus Pugin (1812–52), became one of the dominant features of early Victorian taste.

## Europe and Asia
# Medieval 2

474

**469–475** *Seven details from Owen Jones's influential pattern book* The Grammar of Ornament, *published in 1856. When Jones published these artists' reinterpretations of medieval stained-glass windows – copied from various churches and cathedrals in England and continental Europe – he and his public were interested not so much in history, in what had gone before, but rather in how they could use these 'lost' designs to invigorate Victorian art forms. More specifically, there was a huge upsurge in church building during the Victorian era, and this brought with it a revival in the art and craft of stained glass. So while these images are described as 'medieval', it is important to bear in mind that the shapes and forms have been modified and adjusted to suit Victorian needs. All that said, and not forgetting that many of the original medieval stained-glass windows had been vandalised, rebuilt or sometimes even reinterpreted, these seven designs show how the once clearly defined stem-and-foliage forms (as seen, for example, in no.* **475***) had gradually evolved to the point where the stems had all but disappeared from view and the foliage was reduced to a piece of stylised pattern. The stylised acanthus leaf, reinterpreted from medieval forms, became one of the most popular motifs of the Victorian period.*

471

469

472

470

473

475

476

**476** *A detail from a stained-glass window from the 12th-century Cathedral of Bourges, a city in central France. This pattern beautifully illustrates how the once-dynamic stem-and-foliage pattern, seen particularly in early medieval manuscripts, evolved to the point where the stem had vanished and the foliage was reduced to repeats of the same image. The underlying grid of the design is made up of two elements: the circle and the square. The roundels have been set within the squares in such a way that the waste ground at the corners of neighbouring squares fit together to make a lozenge shape. Within this framework, the pattern details have been reduced to a formula: the quatrefoil motif at the centre of the circle, a single acanthus motif that has been repeatedly mirror-imaged and reversed to fill the rest of the circle, and an infill of acanthus that has been mirror-imaged to fill the remaining lozenge. Victorian taste-makers such as Owen Jones found patterns such as this too static, even 'tired', but to modern eyes the pared-down, screenprint-like design and bold colours are very appealing.*

*Europe and Asia*
# Medieval 3

477

478

479

**477–478** *Two illustrations showing 12th-century encaustic tiles now in the British Museum. While the patterns draw influence from much the same sources as other decorative art forms, the making procedure (which involves rolling the clay over a patterned mold) is such that the lines of the design have to be reduced to broad areas, with a minimum of fine detail. When the 19th-century manufacturer Herbert Minton saw these designs, he reproduced them as quarry tiles in a style that we now think of as being Victorian.*

**479** *This unusual design is based on an intriguing mixture of sources: the ancient swastika motif (a symbol of good luck); mythical beasts such as the griffin and the dragon; and the 13th- and 14th-century interest in geometry, perspective and optical illusion. The design forms part of a mural from a 14th-century French church.*

480

481

482

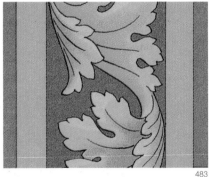

483

484

**480** *A detail from a 14th-century wood-and-ivory inlay design, probably a reinterpretation of a Moorish tile. The pattern has been adapted so that the forms can be worked as a series of straight lines, to suit the technique of wood inlay.*

**481** *This intricate design is made up of small cubes of wood and ivory, a technique known as intarsia. It comes from a 15th-century Italian church.*

**482** *The fleur-de-lys, or lily flower, is a heraldic device of the French royal arms. In this 14th-century French mural border, the rather elongated shape also recalls the much older Persian lily pattern.*

**483–484** *Two painted border details from wall murals in a 14th-century French church. It is interesting to note that while both designs are based on the vine-acanthus theme, one design reduces the forms to stylised, almost abstract blocks of colour, while the other has a semi-realistic effect.*

*Europe and Asia*
# Medieval 4

485

486

487

**485–487** *Three details showing pattern forms from a selection of medieval Italian manuscripts, probably from the late 14th century. They display an intriguing mixture of sources. Medieval 'acanthus'-inspired foliage can be seen in all three, while the upper motif in the pattern on the left (485) is derived from the Celtic knot. However, they are also strongly influenced by Classical sources.*

**488–490** *Three details from late 15th-century Italian manuscripts from* The Grammar of Ornament *published by Owen Jones in 1856. Although the patterns were technically created in the Renaissance, they are included here because the formalised petals of* **488**, *and the odd mix of the natural and the formalised in* **489** *and* **490**, *are developments from the late medieval. Jones's own – very Victorian – view was that conventional stylised ornamentation and artistic realism should not be mixed together.*

488

489

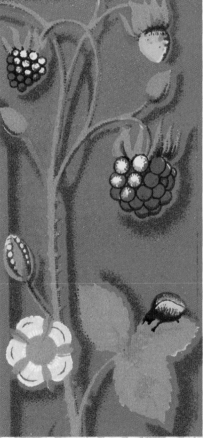

490

## Europe and Asia
# Medieval 5

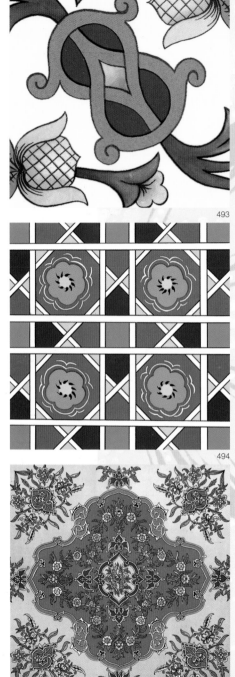

493

491

492

494

495

**491–496** *Six illustration details from a pattern book of historical folk art from Russia and Tadzhikistan. Although these examples were gathered together in the modern era, traditional patterns such as these stretch back to medieval times and remained more or less unchanged for centuries. Tadzhikistan shares its border with Afghanistan, Iran and China, and so it is hardly surprising that designs from this area have much in common with those seen elsewhere in this book. For example, the floral patterns of nos.* **491, 493, 495** *and* **496** *share their mix of formalised floral and geometric shapes and flat areas of colour with some ancient Chinese rugs and embroidery. Nos.* **492** *and* **494** *are both details of 'folk pattern' from the borders of an illustrated children's book, by an unknown Russian artist. Ivan Bilibin, the famous Russian illustrator and artist, believed that the patterns of Central Asia all originated with the nomadic Turkoman rug weavers, who had wandered from the borders of China to India, Tibet and Persia since ancient times.*

*Europe and Asia*
# Medieval 6

**497** *Although this pattern, a mixed
boteh and floral folk-art formula, is
believed to have originated in medieval
times, it is shown here taken from a
French printed textile of the 1820s.
It is interesting for displaying ancient
forms in a more modern context.*

497

**498** *A detail from a woven textile that draws influence from much older designs. In the context of weaving, the 'rediscovery' of the Middle Ages was epitomised by tapestries. This design picks up on older patterns and motifs from Persia and Turkey and presents them in a bold heraldic form that the Victorians thought of as being 'medieval'. This piece was made in Morocco in the mid-19th century.*

**499** *A 19th-century woven textile – from Morocco – that harks back to traditional patterns. The dominant motif is the mihrab, from the Arabic meaning the niche in a mosque that points in the direction of Mecca. However, the small, flat areas of formalised foliage are similar to those on medieval tiles, which are themselves believed to have been influenced by Persian pattern.*

**500** *In an effort to respond to the fashion for medieval revival designs, the weaver of this 19th-century Moroccan textile has incorporated as many traditional patterns as possible. Not content with filling the ground with* boteh *motifs, the weaver has also filled the area within each* boteh *with the* zil-I-soltan *(vase of flowers) motif, which is often found in Persian designs dating from medieval times.*

498

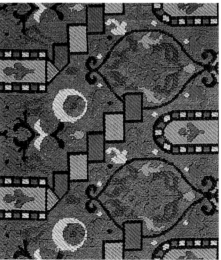

499

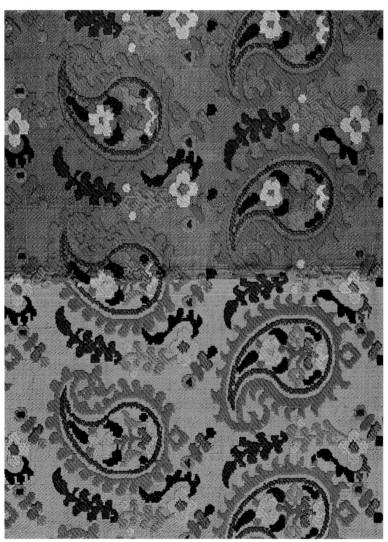

500

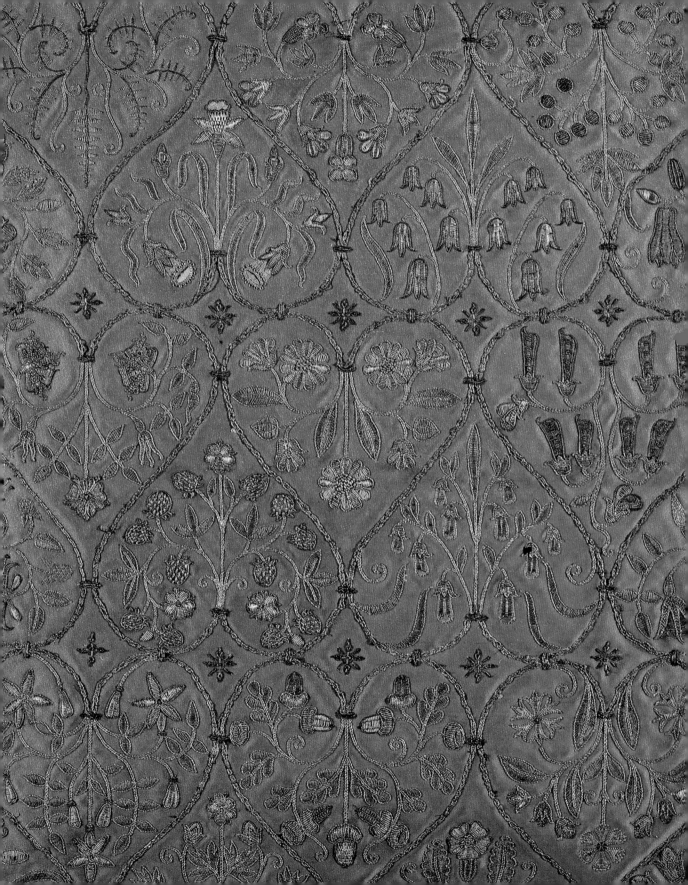

501

502

503

504

## Europe
# Renaissance

**501** *An array of flowers and plants decorates this cushion cover, which was made in London in the late 1500s. Ferns, daisies, daffodils, bellflowers and even acorns can all be seen, delicately embroidered in silk and metallic thread on a fine woven red silk ground. While the flowers themselves are arranged with formal symmetry, they are set within a graceful heart-shaped pattern that shows the influence of Italian Renaissance forms.*

**502–504** *Three details from textiles woven in Lucca, Italy, in the late 14th century. Under the influence of the Crusades, the Sicilian weavers of the 13th and 14th centuries produced many beautiful fabrics enriched with winged lions, foliated crosses and crowns, rayed stars, harts and birds and armorial bearings. This weaving tradition was later introduced into Lucca, where the weavers produced fabrics inspired by the Sicilian originals.*

The Renaissance was characterised by a revival of interest in the art forms of the ancient world. Designers borrowed motifs from the recently discovered remains of Roman sarcophagi and triumphal arches. They also drew inspiration from the paintings found at Nero's *Domus Aurea* ('Golden House') in Rome. These designs, which featured a playful mixture of chimerical monsters, putti (cherubs), vases, cornucopiae and flowing tendrils, became known as 'grotesques'. Renaissance artists also displayed a growing interest in the natural world. Through the study of perspective and anatomy, they found ways of portraying nature more realistically than ever before. This is evident in their sumptuous manuscripts and in ornamental details such as strapwork, which mimicked the appearance of curling leather.

*Europe*
# Renaissance 2

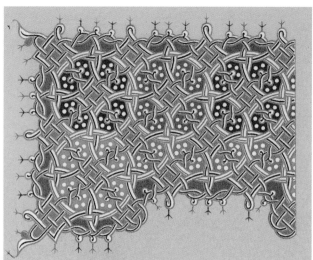

507

508

505

509

506

**505–513** *Nine illustrated details from a selection of 16th-century Russian manuscripts and metalwork. While Russian artists of this period were somewhat nervous about breaking away from past influences – Viking, Celtic, Persian, Chinese, and so forth – they were nevertheless excited about the altogether brighter and lighter Renaissance influences that were sweeping across western Europe. They compromised by reworking their old designs so that they reflected the new ideas – more colour, more control and with a lighter feel. As these designs show, while the Russian designers and artists of the period still favoured the* ancient Viking–Celtic 'magic knot', this traditional motif has been opened up and given a more delicate feel by the addition of little curlicues – such as the stylised leaves, tendrils and flowers seen in nos. **510–513**. If you compare these patterns with earlier Russian designs (see, for example, no. **468**), you will see that they are subtly different. The magic knot is still there, but the writhing snake-like forms have been tidied up and tamed. Artists from the 16th century onwards used the Renaissance drawing implements of compass, square and protractor, and these no doubt led to the traditional designs becoming less frenzied and more controlled.

511

510

512

513

## Europe
# Renaissance 3

**514–516** *Many of the motifs in these three 16th-century designs for stained-glass windows were inspired by or copied from Classical Greek and Roman originals. The half-man and half-beast figure is a common Classical type, as is the winged 'putto' (the small naked boy in no. 515). Other Classically inspired details include urns, a Roman-style medallion, foliate scrolls and acanthus leaves. In nos. 514 and 515 you can also see examples of 'strapwork', a type of ornamentation composed of bands or ribbons. Strapwork was popular in northern Europe and these designs may have come from France.*

**517–519** *Three architectural drawing details showing window surrounds dating from the 16th century, from Yaroslavl – a prosperous trading centre north of Moscow. Russian design pulled together elements from the East and the West. Here, the pointed brickwork takes Eastern forms, while the flat patterns on the painted shutters recall more Western traditions.*

514

515

516

517

518

519

*Europe*
# Renaissance 4

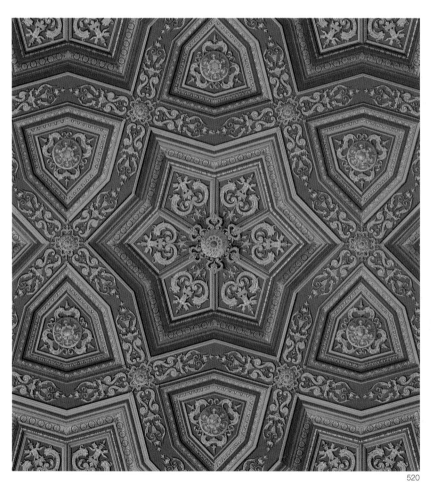

520

521

**520** *A detail from the ceiling in the Palais de Justice, Rouen, northern France, built in the early 1500s. It was just at the close of the 15th century that the influence of the Italian Renaissance began to be felt upon French art. Renaissance design invariably displayed a fascination with geometry – something that is joyously explored in this pattern, where the underlying grid has obviously been created using a compass.*

**521–523** *Three illustrations showing details from French and Italian glass and ceramics, made at the very end of the 15th century. One of the major 'discoveries' of Renaissance artists was the accurate portrayal of perspective and three-dimensional form, and the artist responsible for the design on the left, no. **521**, no doubt wanted to show off this skill. Nos. **522** and **523** combine three-dimensional modelling with 'grotesque' elements (named after the Classical decoration found in submerged Roman ruins, or 'grottoes') such as ribbons, swags, scrolls, mythical figures and delicately intertwined stems and leaves.*

522

523

**524–525** *Two details from a French Book of Hours made in the first half of the 16th century. While these designs look back to the medieval themes of hunting and harvest, the lifelike figures, with their natural-looking poses, show the influence of Italian Renaissance artists.*

**526–527** *While these two designs feature Renaissance-style medallions complete with foliated tracery, the overall theme draws inspiration from the jewel-encrusted covers of medieval manuscripts. Both details come from the decorated cover of an Italian illuminated manuscript, made in the early 15th century.*

*Europe*
# Renaissance 5

524

525

526

527

528

529

**528–529** *These two illustrations –
details copied from Raphael's
famous frescoes in the Vatican,
created in the early 16th century
– show the Renaissance love of
Roman-style ornament. The swags
and ribbons, the fluted urns, the
columns, the half-man half-beast
figures and the playful putti are
all familiar to us from bronzes
and wall decorations found in the
Roman city of Pompeii. Raphael,
of course, would not have known
about Pompeii, which was not
excavated until the 18th century,
but he would certainly have been
fascinated by the then-recent
Roman discoveries of the Bath of
Titus and House of Livia, with
their beautiful mural paintings.*

**530–534** *A selection of margin
decorations from a late 16th-
century Italian manuscript. These
designs mix stylised Classical
ornament – scrolls, acanthus leaves,
Roman-style medallions, even the
head of a mythical beast – with
realistic portraits and paintings
from nature. Butterflies, caterpillars
and even a snail are among the
delicately painted details.*

530     531     532     533     534

*Europe*
# Renaissance 6

536

537

535

538

**535** *The beautifully direct and naive pattern on this piece of 16th-century earthenware pottery is achieved by a technique called* sgraffito – *the scratching through one layer of glaze or slip to reveal the colour of an underlying layer. While this example is probably French, much the same techniques were used in Italy and England at this time.*

**536–537** *Two details from a piece of late 15th-century maiolica (tin-glaze) pottery. The character of the pattern – the foliated 'S' forms and the button studs – suggests that the potter drew inspiration from a tapestry or perhaps a painting detail featuring a curtain or drape. The colours suggest that this piece of pottery comes from northern Italy.*

**538** *Many traditional folk designs were untouched by the Classical revival of the Renaissance. Peasant wares such as this maiolica jug were part of an ongoing tradition, and designs remained unchanged over the years. The simple decoration was achieved by brush-painting with metallic oxides on top of a tin glaze.*

**539** *This design has its beginnings in the Egyptian cartouche – a round-ended oblong shape enclosing characters expressing royal or divine names in Egyptian hieroglyphics. The detail comes from a piece of 17th-century French porcelain.*

**540, 542** *Stylised flowers set within a diagonal grid form the basis for these two design details, taken from pieces of 16th-century Italian peasant pottery. While sophisticated styles – such as the Renaissance fashion for Classical forms – came and went, there remained an underlying and ongoing folk tradition. Of course new techniques evolve, and colours and glazes are specific to different regions, but to a great extent naive pattern forms such as this are very slow to change.*

**541** *A detail from a piece of 16th-century French enamel. While this piece is made from metal and glaze, the designs drew their inspiration from a woodcarved original – probably a detail from a panel or a piece of furniture. This is borne out by the fact that the tongue-like leaf detail, and the dot-and-dash border, are all gouge-worked forms as used by the woodcarver.*

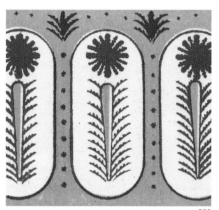

539

541

540

542

543

544

545

546

**543** *This design nicely catalogues many of the motifs that characterise the late Baroque period. Almost everything is present: the winged mask, the putti (angelic children), the abundance of fruit and birds and, perhaps most characteristic of all, the half-woman, half-beast caryatid-cum-satyr (bottom centre). This detail comes from the cover of an Italian manuscript made in the second half of the 16th century.*

**544–546** *Three illustrations of 17th- and 18th-century French tapestries. The patterns were intended to fool the eye into believing that the wall was elaborately carved and painted – a sort of* trompe-l'oeil *effect. To this end, the designers have used imagery that has its origins in woodcarving. For example, the ornate egg-and-tongue detailing and sweeping foliage in pattern* **544** *look as though they have been worked with a woodworker's gouge.*

## *Europe*
# Baroque & Rococo

The word 'Baroque' is thought to be derived from the Portuguese word for a rough or irregularly shaped pearl. The style reached its peak in the 17th century and was notable for its grandeur, its dynamism and its taste for theatrical effects. It retained many of the motifs that had become popular during the Renaissance – putti, acanthus, exuberant scrollwork – but deployed them in a weightier and more monumental manner. If Baroque was the ideal style for decorating palaces, then Rococo was more suited to the boudoir. Taking its name from the French word *rocaille* (fancy rockwork), it was light, elegant, playful, sometimes even erotic. Shells, arabesques and scrollwork were the most popular motifs, and these were often accompanied by the trappings of pastoral idylls.

*Europe*
# Baroque & Rococo 2

**547–554** *Baroque scrolls, masks, cartouches (frames) and other classically inspired motifs abound in these eight details, all taken from a late 17th-century console table. The table was made in France by the famous cabinet-maker André Charles Boulle, who had a studio workshop in the Louvre and made furniture exclusively for King Louis XIV. Boulle specialised in elaborate marquetry, such as this example, and even developed his own 'secret' technique. This involved stacking together the sheet materials – wood, ivory, metal – then cutting out the motifs through all the layers. The pieces of the resulting jigsaw puzzle were then counterchanged. Boulle's technique was labour-saving and cut his material costs in half. His system of applying marquetry was not new – the Egyptians had used similar techniques – but it was Boulle who developed it and popularised it in France, where it was used*

547

548

549

550

throughout the 17th and 18th centuries. The style was enormously influential, with designers, jewellers and decorators from across Europe imitating Boulle's pattern forms. The term 'Boulle work' is now used to describe just about any form of elaborate marquetry from this period.

551

552

553

554

*Europe*
# Baroque
# & Rococo 3

**555–557** *Three 18th-century cartouches (ornamental frames): 555 and 556 from France and 557 from Germany. These three examples nicely show the difference between the Baroque and Rococo styles. While they* are all based to some extent on rock and shell forms, the Baroque (**557**) is above all ordered and symmetrical, while the Rococo goes out of its way to be asymmetrical.

**558** *A detail from a tapestry made in France in the 18th century. This design, complete with foliated scrolls and flowers, pastoral scenes and harvest implements, is a good example of what came to be called the 'transitional Baroque–Rococo style'. The Rococo style, an elaboration of the Baroque, is characterised by frivolous details, especially by the rocks and shells that gave it its name.*

558

555

559

560

561

556

557

562

**559–562** *The patterns and motifs on these details – from a French 18th-century wall panel – are good examples of the rather heavy Baroque style that gave life to Rococo forms. The archaeological discoveries of the period resulted in designs that drew inspiration from ancient Greek and Roman forms, as borne out by the foliated scrolls and the urns with swags to the side.*

**563–564** *Two details from carved and gilt wall panels from the Palace of Versailles, France. These panels have all the characteristic motifs of Rococo. There are scrolls, shells and flowers, and tools associated with the pastoral life, all arranged in an asymmetrical group. While 18th-century champions of the Rococo described it as 'playful, glittering, feminine … full of vegetables and leaves of every kind … tendrils, shells and musical instruments, … so much pleasure …', critics described it as '…unnatural, excess to excess … a kind of vertigo.'*

563

564

The patterns in this section begin in the 19th century when the expansion of the middle classes produced a huge rise in demand for decoration with which to furnish their homes and therefore affirm their economic and social status and respectability. By the 1860s machines for the mass production of wallpapers and textiles were in place in all of the larger centres of manufacturing in Europe and the United States. At first this resulted in crudely coloured

and misaligned prints, which gave rise to the Movement for Design Reform and the influential Arts and Crafts Exhibition Society led by William Morris, who campaigned for a return to the craftsmanship of hand-generated ornamentation. However, this movement was thwarted by the relentless rise in technical invention and improvements. In particular, the

## Part Two
# Post-Industrial

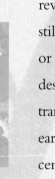

widespread acceptance of easily used and brightly coloured, chemically synthesised dyestuffs revolutionised the use of colour. Patterns are still based on floral motifs, whether naturalistic or stylised, but also on geometric or abstract designs inspired by modern forms of architecture, transport, machinery and art movements of the early 20th century. Towards the end of the 20th century, the development of new production methods and advances in fabric and paper technology led to larger-scale and more intricate designs. These innovations look set to continue with digitally manipulated surface-pattern designs, often generated entirely on the computer.

## *Europe*
# 19th Century

**565** *The synthetic chemical dyes introduced in the 19th century opened up all sorts of opportunities for textile designers and printers. The brilliantly coloured, larger-than-life pattern on this roller-printed fabric, made in 1850, exploits these new techniques.*

566

**566** *A detail from an 1815 block-printed 'Island' fabric, probably American. The name comes from the way that the motifs are printed as separate pictures on a plain ground, like islands.*

**567** *'Pillar' prints such as this, featuring classical pillars topped with flowers, were popular in the early 19th century. This roller-printed fabric was made in England in 1820 for the American market.*

567

**568** *The figurative style of this late-18th-century fabric looks forward to 19th-century prints. The design was adapted from an engraving by Jean-François Janinet, which was in turn inspired by a musical comedy.*

568

The 19th century witnessed a new appreciation of design and the decorative arts. These were promoted through a series of influential, international shows, such as Britain's Great Exhibition of 1851 and France's Universal Exhibitions (from 1855). In the United States there were similar displays at the Philadelphia 1876 Exhibition and Chicago's Columbian Exposition of 1893. The broad scope of these shows encouraged a greater eclecticism in the work of designers as they experimented with foreign styles while also reassessing the art of the past. Many older patterns were revived during the 19th century, one of the most notable examples being tartan. This had been outlawed after the Jacobite uprising of 1745, but its fortunes were restored, following the success of George IV's state visit to Scotland in 1822.

*Europe*
# 19th
# Century 2

**569** *A detail from a tiled wainscot (the lower part of an internal wall), made in England in the late 19th century. A profusion of styles coexisted in Victorian England, but one of the most fashionable was the medieval or Gothic revival. The red tiles seen here draw inspiration from a tile designed by Augustus Pugin in 1848, which in turn had been inspired by English medieval encaustic tiles.*

**570–572** *Three panels made from late 19th-century Spanish tesselated tiles. They draw inspiration from Greek, Roman, Etruscan, Moorish and Egyptian sources – from the tiles and pavements that were being unearthed in the last quarter of the 19th century. These same sources were later to influence the Art Deco style.*

**573** *With its bold, geometrical design, this early 20th-century tile panel seems to look forward to the Art Deco style of the 1920s. Like patterns 570–572, it fuses various exotic sources.*

**574** *When this tiled panel was created in England in the late 19th century, designers were both harking back to old traditions and looking outwards to those of other countries and cultures. The designer of this panel brought together two quite different traditions. The large motif at the centre is an interpretation of a medieval motif,*

569

572

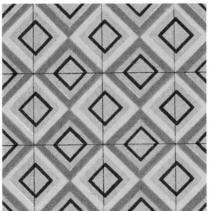

570

573

571

574

575

577

576

578

while the repeat tiles draw inspiration from traditional Japanese textiles.

**575–576** *Two details from a Russian house, built in 1876. The walls feature 'diaper' brick designs – patterns made using different-coloured bricks. While these patterns certainly hark back to traditional Russian architectural styles, designs of this character were predominantly the result of 19th-century improvements in brick manufacture – bigger kilns, greater control over firing temperature, and so on. Polychrome brick patterns were popular in many northern European countries over this period.*

**577–578** *Tiled panels with occasional feature tiles were especially popular in Victorian England. These two 19th-century wainscot panels are manufacturers' samples; with their mixture of patterns and styles, they were probably an attempt to sell off back-catalogue designs.*

*Europe*
# 19th
# Century 3

579

580

**579–586** *Eight details from a late 19th-century English pattern book that drew inspiration from a whole range of historical sources – including the folk American sunflower, the Persian tulip, the European daisy, the classical Roman vine and the North African palm. The designs top left (**579**) and far right (**582–586**) are interesting in that while they are all drawn directly from examples of wood and ivory inlay, the illustrator has greatly changed the balance of the design in some patterns by enlarging the ivory fixing pins, to the extent that they are now a significant part of the overall pattern. The patterns bottom left (**580**) and near right (**581**) provide an interesting demonstration of how it is possible to derive very different patterns from the same source. They both draw inspiration from a five-petaled flower – showing both side and front views – and yet one designer has gone for the single triangular image while the other has chosen a stylised flower-like image that is itself made up of both front and side views.*

581

582

583

584

585

586

*Europe*
# 19th
# Century 4

588

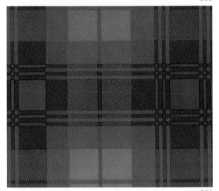

589

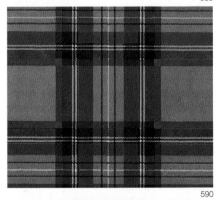

590

587

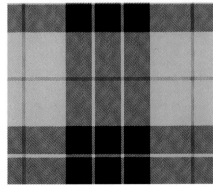

591

**587–595** *Nine details showing traditional Scottish tartans from James Grant's influential book* The Tartans of the Clans of Scotland, *first published in 1886. On the left,* **587** *is 'Sinclair' tartan, while* **588–591** *are 'MacPherson Hunting' tartan, 'Macnab' tartan, 'Royal Stuart' tartan and 'MacLeod' tartan respectively. On this page,* **592** *is a 'Jacobite' tartan,* **593** *is an 'Old Stuart',* **594** *is 'Buchan' tartan and* **595** *is 'Stewart Hunting'. While loom-woven tartans were made in ancient times – borne out by scraps found in various tombs – the notion of each clan having its own identifiable tartan pattern is relatively new.*

*Though some experts disagree, the likelihood is that the idea of each clan having its own weave began in the early 1800s. Of course village weavers would have had individual styles, used natural colours that were local to their area and favoured different arrangements of warp and weft, but these differences were never documented. The experts who claim that clan tartans were invented in the early years of the 19th century cite as their proof the fact that while there are many old and very detailed accounts that describe battles between clans, and battles between the clans and the English, none of these accounts mentions tartan. Today new tartans are invented and registered every year. There are Canadian tartans, American tartans, Northern English tartans, Welsh tartans and Cornish tartans.*

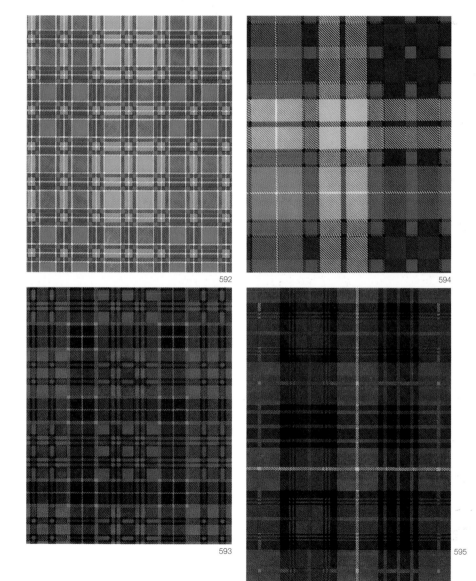

592

594

593

595

596

597

598

599

**596** *'Strawberry Thief' was one of William Morris's most successful fabric designs. It was designed in 1883 and sold through his firm Morris & Co. The pattern was inspired by the problem at Kelmscott, Morris's country house, of how to keep the thrushes off the strawberries.*

**597** *'Trellis' was the first wallpaper that William Morris designed, in 1862. It was not registered until two years later, however, after two other designs. It was a personal favourite: Morris used it to decorate his daughter May's nursery.*

**598** *The British designer Christopher Dresser was passionately interested in botany and in Japanese art. Both influences can be seen in this printed cotton fabric, which dates from 1899.*

**599** *A detail from a woven fabric, 'Purple Bird', designed in 1899 by C. F. A. Voysey, one of the prime movers of Arts and Crafts style.*

## Europe
# Arts & Crafts

This movement takes its name from the Arts and Crafts Exhibition Society founded in England in 1888 by William Morris, Lewis F. Day and others, to promote the decorative arts. Their designs are complex, often featuring pattern on pattern, and were influenced by medieval European tapestries and textiles as well as by the Gothic Revival ornament of the time. Arts and Crafts artists relied heavily on the natural world for their imagery. Native birds were a popular motif, appearing within pastoral scenes. Lilies, honeysuckle, jasmine and daisies were among the flowers depicted. William Morris revitalised the arts of block-printing and natural dyeing, using plant dyes to produce the soft, harmonising palette of earthy reds, blues, ochres and soft greens that has become an essential part of the colour vocabulary we enjoy today.

*Europe*
# Arts & Crafts 2

600

**600** *Rendered in flat blocks of colour, the simplified botanical forms on this pattern owe an obvious debt to Japanese art. It was created in 1899 by Christopher Dresser, who produced numerous innovative designs for textiles, glass, ceramics, wallpapers, metalwork, woodwork and graphics.*

**601** *John Henry Dearle made this printed cotton, called 'Compton', in 1896. It displays all the typical attributes of Arts and Crafts textile design: the muted colour palette, the swirling floral motifs and the layers of pattern on pattern. Dearle was one of William Morris's assistants and became manager of Morris's firm after his death.*

**602** *The bold simplicity and glowing colours of this printed cotton fabric are typical of the work of M. H. Baillie Scott, who designed it in 1905. Scott was an architect as well as a designer; he built many houses in a simple, rustic style.*

**603** *A book-binding design by William Morris, made in the late 1880s. It is a reworking of a 16th-century pattern.*

**604** *A detail from a woven silk-and-wool cloth, made about 1898 by C. F. A. Voysey for Alexander Morton & Co. The design was influenced by Voysey's interest in Japanese art and in the restraints imposed by weaving techniques.*

**605** *Designed by Christopher Dresser in 1899, this delicately drawn cotton fabric, ornamented with formalised irises, demonstrates once more Dresser's interest in botany and Japanese art. Dresser, unlike many of his contemporaries, was fully attuned to the needs of machine production.*

**606** *A detail from a printed velvet fabric, inspired by traditional Japanese art. It was made in 1888 by L. F. Day, a founder member of the Arts and Crafts Exhibition Society.*

601

604

602

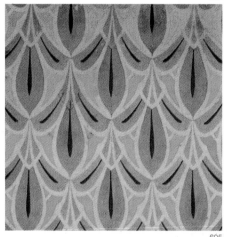

605

603

606

*Europe*
# Arts & Crafts 3

**607** *This William Morris design features densely packed, naturalistic flowers and foliage, rendered in muted, earthy colours. This detail comes from a wool-and-silk tapestry – Morris began to experiment with tapestry-weaving in 1878. Highly time-consuming to make, tapestries such as this were produced at the Morris & Co. workshops in Merton Abbey.*

**608** *A William Morris wallpaper design entitled 'Apple', made about 1875. As far as Morris was concerned a good wallpaper was acceptable as a substitute for a painted wall or fresco. That said, his thinking was that if you couldn't have a first-class wallpaper then it was best to settle for a plain whitewashed wall.*

608

609

607

610

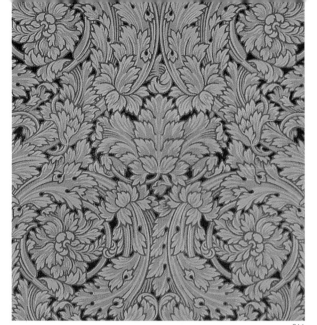

611

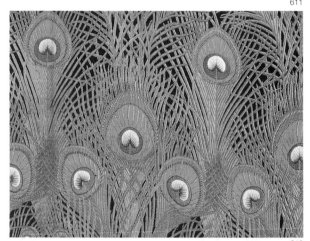

612

613

**609** *This textile by British designer Harry Napper is a good demonstration of the crossover between Arts and Crafts and the continental Art Nouveau style (see page 225). The fabric was made about 1887 and was sold through the influential London store Liberty & Co. Napper designed wallpapers as well as textiles.*

**610** *'Cromer Bird', designed by A. H. Mackmurdo. The fluid, flowing forms draw their inspiration from traditional Japanese art and from the work of the painter and poet William Blake. Mackmurdo was founder of the Century Guild, the stated aim of which was 'to render all branches of art the sphere no longer of the tradesman but the artist'. He went on to become one of the prime exponents of the European Art Nouveau style.*

**611** *Probably for a wallpaper, this design was created in 1894 by Lewis Foreman Day. An educator and journalist as well as a designer, Day produced furniture, jewellery, stained glass and silverware alongside a wide range of wall-papers and textiles.*

**612** *The peacock feather, a motif borrowed from Indian art, is the instantly recognisable hallmark of Liberty & Co. This department store was at the forefront of progressive design in the 1880s and 1890s and helped to create a fashion for Eastern-imported goods as well as for Art Nouveau. This printed cotton fabric, called 'Peacock Feather', was made for Liberty's by the English designer Arthur Silver. His firm, Silver Studio, specialised in printed wallpapers and textiles, sold directly to stores such as Liberty's.*

**613** *With its flattened, two-dimensional forms and clear, uncluttered appearance, this block-printed textile design anticipates the work of the Wiener Werkstätte artists at the beginning of the 20th century (see page 239). Entitled 'Honesty', it was made by Lindsay Phillip Butterfield about 1898. Butterfield designed numerous wallpapers and fabrics for companies such as Liberty's and Sanderson's.*

*Europe*
# Arts & Crafts 4

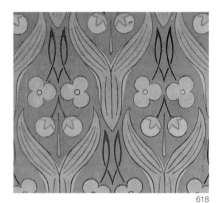

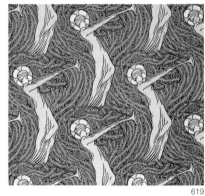

**614** *A detail from the 'Dove and Rose' fabric designed by William Morris in 1879. Morris sent this design to Scotland to be woven by Alexander Morton & Co. When asked about the quality of this fabric, Morris said, '… It will last as long as need be, since the cloth is really strong. I can't answer so decidedly as to the colour…'*

**615** *Birds, leaves and tulip-like flowers are drawn in a typically two-dimensional manner in this textile design by C. F. A. Voysey, made about 1895. The repeat design demonstrates Voysey's stated ideals of 'Simplicity, sincerity, repose, directness and frankness'. Voysey also designed furniture, cutlery and lighting.*

**616** *The first colour run of William Morris's 'Kennet', a printed cotton cloth produced about 1883. Morris produced this design in many different forms, including velveteen, woven cotton and woven silk.*

**617** *A detail from a design, possibly by C. F. A. Voysey, made about 1890. While the flatness of the shapes is*

620

622

621

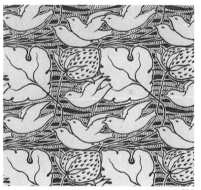

623

**620** *A detail from a William Morris design for a printed cotton, made in 1883 and entitled 'Wey'. Morris was so pleased with the structure of the flowerhead motifs that he used similar forms in later designs: the 'Wandle' chintz in 1884; the 'Windrush' wallpaper in 1883; and others.*

**621** *Brightly coloured and highly naturalistic, this rather uncharacteristic design was made by Arthur Silver at Silver Studio about 1890. The studio, concentrating on designs for wallpapers and textiles, sold designs to a number of manufacturers and directly to stores, especially to Liberty's.*

**622** *A William Morris design for a hand-printed wallpaper, 'Bruges', made about 1888. Morris made several of these flat, two-tone designs, including one called 'Borage', which he printed as a wallpaper and as a lining fabric for curtains.*

**623** *A design for a printed cotton by C. F. A. Voysey, probably 1898, inspired by traditional Japanese art. If you compare this with pattern* **615** *you will see that in many ways the two designs are very similar in structure and content. Voysey liked to revisit and rework favourite themes until he felt that he had exhausted all their possibilities.*

*typical of Voysey, the entwined leaves, dotted stems and 'layered' design recall the work of William Morris.*

**618** *A design by Christopher Dresser, produced about 1892. While the trefoil shapes recall medieval art, the crisply cut lines of the drawing bear witness to his interest in Japanese printing techniques.*

**619** *This fabric, called 'The Angel with the Trumpet', was designed by Herbert Horne in 1884. It was produced as both a 'cretonne' (strong cotton) and a velveteen. The lithe figures recall those found in contemporary poster designs. Horne was a member of the Century Guild, where he worked in partnership with A. H. Mackmurdo.*

*Europe*
# Arts & Crafts 5

624

625

627

626

628

**624** *Made about 1864, this delicate William Morris wallpaper, plainly drawing from medieval illumination and called 'Daisy', was the firm's bestseller for 50 years.*

**625** *'Anemone', one of William Morris's favourite patterns. The design is printed on a dense weave – ideal for curtains, hangings and upholstery.*

**626** *'Granada', a detail from William Morris's reworking of old Flemish velvet. It proved so costly to make that production was swiftly called to a halt.*

**627** *'Bullers Wood', a design for a carpet by William Morris. While Morris & Co.'s carpets were hugely expensive, they were in great demand by wealthy clients.*

**628** *'St. James', a detail from a woven silk damask cloth designed by William Morris and produced by J. O. Nicholson of Macclesfield.*

**629** *Various beasts are hidden amid swirling foliage in 'The Grotesque', designed by L. F. Day in 1889. Day was one of the founding members of the Arts and Crafts Exhibition Society.*

**630** *A curious pointed flower sits on the centre-line of this strictly mirror-imaged design. It is very possibly by Morris's manager J. H. Dearle.*

**631** *William Morris was passionately fond of sitting in his garden and drawing birds from life. 'Bird and Anemone' dates from 1882.*

**632** *A William Morris design made about 1883. This probably belongs to the series of 'River' chintzes that were produced by Morris in the late 1880s. Morris's daughter May described later in life how her father drew inspiration from a boating trip along the Thames.*

**633** *Stylised peacocks, a popular Eastern motif, form the allover pattern for a block-printed fabric designed by M. H. Baillie Scott about 1905.*

**634** *'Bexley', a woven silk designed in the 1880s by A. H. Mackmurdo for the Century Guild. The flowing lines anticipate the Art Nouveau style.*

*Europe*
# Arts & Crafts 6

**635** *Flowers and foliage are densely packed in this highly detailed William Morris design of about 1884. Entitled 'Wandle', it was inspired by material that Morris saw at the Victoria & Albert Museum. He once said: 'Perhaps I have used the museum as much as any man living'.*

**636** *Typically English flowers are a recurring motif in William Morris's designs. This fabric, 'Honeysuckle', was made in 1876. Along with 'Tulip', produced in 1875, and 'Snakeshead', made the following year, it was one of Morris's bestselling designs.*

**637** *'Snakeshead' by William Morris, designed in 1876 as a printed cotton fabric. This design drew inspiration from the wild-flowers native to the water meadows of Oxford. 'Snakeshead' is one of Morris's best-known patterns and was also one of the designer's own favourites.*

**638** *Another version of 'Bird and Anemone' (see **631**, page 219) designed by William Morris in 1882. The design was used first as a printed cotton and later as a wallpaper. This design was one of Morris's own favourites, was produced in a wide variety of colourways and is still in production today.*

**639** *Thirty different printing blocks are used to achieve the subtle grading of colours in this William Morris wallpaper. Called 'Acanthus', it dates from about 1875.*

**640** *A design for a printed cotton, 'Brother Rabbit' or 'Brer Rabbit', made by William Morris in 1881. This pattern was a tribute to the Uncle Remus stories – a favourite with his daughters, Jane (always called Jenny) and Mary (called May).*

**641** *Bold, red, naturalistically drawn poppies dominate a warm, rich pattern printed on velvet. The fabric was made about 1888 by Thomas Wardle and Co., England.*

635

637

639

636

638

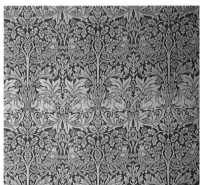

640

*Europe*
# Arts & Crafts 7

**642** *Scrolling tendrils, flowers and foliage in muted colours form a 'turnover' pattern: the motifs and forms turn over mirror-wise around a vertical axis. This design by William Morris, entitled 'Lodden', was produced as a printed cotton fabric about 1884.*

**643** *A detail from a William Morris design. While the title and date are unknown, it is very probably one of the preliminary designs for his 'Forest' tapestry, made in 1887 and shown at the 1890 Arts and Crafts Exhibition.*

**644** *'Vine', a William Morris wallpaper design, made in 1873. The design is based on close observation of the way that plants grow and meander. Morris said of this design that it was a good choice for anyone wanting to soften the lines of an otherwise stiff and formal room.*

**645** *Stylised flowers, buds and leaves are rendered in delicate shades in this 1905 fabric, designed by L. P. Butterfield for G. P. & J. Baker Ltd.*

**646** *Generously proportioned blooms feature on this 1896 design by C. F. A. Voysey. The detail comes from a woven strip of silk-and-wool double-cloth.*

**647** *A William Morris design entitled 'African Marigold' for a printed cotton fabric, made about 1876. This design uses the vertical turnover structure, whereby the motifs are repeated by being mirror-imaged around a vertical axis.*

**648** *An array of earthy brown tones feature in this woven wool tapestry by William Morris, entitled 'Tulip and Rose'. The structure of the pattern is characteristically built by mirror-imaging the motifs around a vertical axis. This design appeared in an 1897 book entitled* The Art of William Morris, *published by George Bell & Sons.*

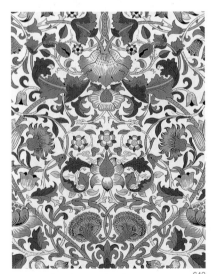

642

643

644

645

646

647

# Europe and America
# Art Nouveau

**649** *The meandering stems and graceful, stylised forms typical of Art Nouveau can be clearly seen in this detail from a woven silk, cotton, and wool cloth. It was created by the wallpaper and textile designer Harry Napper in the late 1890s.*

**650** *A design made by Lewis Foreman Day in 1905. The flower shapes and the flat areas of colour are reminiscent of Japanese prints. Day had been a founder member of the Arts and Crafts Exhibition Society in 1888.*

**651** *'Thistle', a design for a printed cotton by Harry Napper made about 1900. The red flower motifs draw inspiration from those drawn by Charles Rennie Mackintosh, who in turn had taken them from Japanese family-crest motifs.*

**652** *A detail from a design by Eugène Grasset, the Swiss designer and illustrator, for his 1897 book* La plante et ses applications ornamentales.

Art Nouveau grew out of the Arts and Crafts movement and flourished in Europe and the United States. It was strongly influenced by traditional Japanese decorative arts. The recurring motif of a stem meandering from side to side, with its increasingly energetic and 'whiplash' lines, became associated with the Art Nouveau style. Most patterns comprise graceful, highly stylised flowers and foliage, but allegorical scenes, landscapes and seascapes also feature. These intricate designs were characterised by an apparently free fluidity of line that was built on a studied asymmetrical basis. A great significance was put on to the contours, either as outlines or as sinuous stems and entwining tendrils and plants, especially roses, irises and tulips, were frequently combined with a strong vertical emphasis.

*Europe and America*
# Art Nouveau 2

653

656

654

657

655

658

659

**653** 'Gourd' by Eugène Grasset, a detail from his pattern book La plante et ses applications ornamentales. *This influential book comprised 72 coloured plates illustrating usages of plant ornament throughout the decorative arts. Grasset was an important figure in Art Nouveau, who produced a large body of work including posters, stained glass and jewellery.*

**654** *A detail from 'Chestnut Tree', by Eugène Grasset. This design is interesting in that it is a more naturalistic interpretation of natural form than is often found in Art Nouveau, which tends toward stylised pattern. Grasset himself said that simply copying nature was not the way; rather, the artist needed to repeatedly accentuate colours and forms.*

**655** *A detail from a printed silk fabric produced by the Silver Studio about 1900. The motifs begin to show the writhing 'whiplash' forms seen in characteristic Art Nouveau patterns.*

**656** *Leaves and berries are rendered as flat cut-outs in this detail from a design by Eugène Grasset. The motifs were no doubt influenced by Grasset's childhood interest in paper cuts and by his father's work as a sculptor and wood inlayer.*

**657** *A detail from a design, possibly by Eugène Grasset, made in the late 1890s. This design picks up on two motifs favoured by Japanese textile printers: the stylised bird – probably a sparrow – and the hexagon. Note how the pattern cleverly uses a repeat of the bird set within an equilateral triangle.*

**658** 'Dandelion', *a detail from Eugène Grasset's pattern book. The falling seed motif – both the way it is drawn and the way it fits the grid – was inspired by Japanese art in general and stencil-printing techniques in particular.*

**659** *This curious design,* 'Lobsters', *was collected by Hanns Anker and Julius Klinger for their pattern book* La ligne grotesque et ses variations dans la décoration moderne, *published in Paris at the beginning of the 20th century. The original publication included a hinged mirror so that the viewer could see variations of the designs.*

**660** *The elegant shape of these irises and the whiplash reflections in the water were directly inspired by Japanese art. This printed velvet fabric was designed by Félix Aubert in France in 1897.*

*Europe and America*
# Art Nouveau 3

**661** *The iris was a favourite motif of Art Nouveau designers, both because of its interesting form – it is a rewarding plant to draw, with many curly vertical details – and because of its popularity with Japanese artists. This detail comes from a design by Eugène Grasset.*

**662** *A detail from a design by Eugène Grasset entitled 'Sorb', published in 1897. The sorb-apple or service tree was a favourite subject with Grasset. He used it as a centrepiece motif and as small border details.*

**663** *A detail from a printed cotton fabric, produced by F. Steiner & Co. about 1903. Steiner used top designers and produced many high-quality Art Nouveau fabrics.*

**664** *Another Eugène Grasset design, entitled 'Sunflowers', published in 1897. The sunflower has long been a favourite subject for artists the world over. But while many would be drawn to the flower's vibrant colour, for the Art Nouveau designer the interest lies in the shapely forms of petals, buds and leaves.*

661

664

662

665

663

666

667

668

669

**665** *'Nasturtium', a design by Eugène Grasset published in 1897. Art Nouveau artists particularly favoured plants with tendrils, and the nasturtium worked perfectly in the style.*

**666** *Ladybirds form the unusual motif for this French design. The 'bird's-eye view' is, again, inspired by Japanese work.*

**667** *A detail from a French wallpaper design entitled 'Five-Leaved Ivy', produced in 1897. Note the characteristic whiplash form of the tendrils.*

**668** *'Carp', a design collected by Hanns Anker and Julius Klinger for their pattern book* La ligne grotesque et ses variations dans la décoration moderne. *The design draws inspiration from Eastern art, in which carp are a lucky motif.*

**669** *An unusual hybrid, this French pattern has a foreground of stylised daffodils (common in the Art Nouveau repertoire of flowers) with stencil-like outlines and a trellis background which recalls some of the Chinese-style lattices of mid-19th-century patterns.*

*Europe and America*
# Art Nouveau 4

**670** *Delicate orange-coloured flowerheads stand out upon an almost monochrome background. This detail comes from* La plante et ses applications ornamentales, *by the Swiss designer and illustrator Eugène Grasset, published in 1897. Grasset was like William Morris in that he believed passionately that art should be a joy as much for the maker as the user.*

**671** *Pastel colours and gently curving plants, like fronds drifting in a meandering stream, perfectly characterise the slightly cooler English Art Nouveau style. This detail comes from a printed fabric produced by F. Steiner & Co. in 1903.*

670

671

**672** *A vibrantly coloured design by Harry Napper, made about 1907. Napper worked for the Silver Studio, designing everything from wallpapers and fabrics through carpets, embroideries, metalwork and furniture. His work was equally favoured in England and on the Continent.*

**673** *'Fish in Waves', a design collected by Hanns Anker and Julius Klinger for their pattern book* La ligne grotesque et ses variations dans la décoration moderne. *The curling wave forms would have greatly appealed to Art Nouveau designers. The design is strongly derived from motifs seen on traditional Japanese stencil-printed textiles.*

**674** *A detail from a roller-printed cotton velvet, designer unknown, made in France about 1901. The technique of mirror-imaging plant forms on a vertical axis to create a single high-shouldered symmetrical motif was a trick used by Art Nouveau artists. Some artists actually used mirrors to help them achieve their designs.*

**675** *A design for wallpaper made in 1897 by the Swiss designer and illustrator Eugène Grasset. Grasset visited Egypt in 1869 and subsequently*

*moved to Paris. Here he began designing textiles, ornamental letters and then posters. He was especially inspired by Japanese prints, such as those by Hiroshige and Hokusai. It is ironic that Grasset's work has come to characterise Art Nouveau, as he claimed that it was a style that he intensely disliked.*

**676** *Eugène Grasset's style is often more restrained than that of his contemporaries. Avoiding characteristic swirling fronds and meandering tendrils, this design for a poster border draws on the simplified forms of Japanese art.*

672

674

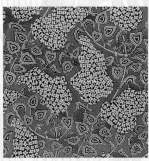

675

673

676

*Europe and America*
# Art Nouveau 5

677

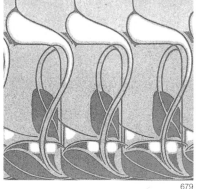

678

679

680

681

**677** *'Wisteria' by Eugène Grasset. With its thick black lines this design recalls stained glass, a popular medium for Art Nouveau artists.*

**678** *This illustration, 'Water-Lily', looks very much like an interpretation from a paper cut-out stencil plate, with simplified flowers and leaves and crisply delineated outlines.*

**679–680** *Two wall decorations by R. Beauclair, made about 1902. Both designs pick up on the drawn-out trumpet-like motif that came to characterise Art Nouveau design.*

**681** *The poet Louis Aragon said of Art Nouveau: 'The whole fauna of human fantasies, their marine vegetation, drifts and luxuriates in the dimly lit zones*

*of human activity'. There could hardly be a more apt description of this early 20th-century French fabric.*

**682** *A detail from a printed cotton, produced in 1902 by F. Steiner & Co. The squared-up tulip head and the rigid vertical–horizontal grid suggest the influence of the Scottish designer Charles Rennie Mackintosh.*

682

686

683

685

687

**683** *'Five-Leaved Ivy', a border detail from a design by Eugène Grasset. When Grasset moved to Paris, he used motifs of just this character in his celebrated covers for* Harper's Bazaar.

**684** *A fantasy world of pattern and colour is conjured up by this 1902 cotton fabric by F. Steiner & Co.*

*It is easy to see why designs such as this appealed to the 'psychedelia' generation of the 1960s.*

**685** *The peacock was a favourite Art Nouveau motif, borrowed from Indian and Japanese art. This design was produced by Eugène Grasset in the last years of the 19th century.*

**686** *The forms in this 1905 tile design are naively drawn and blockily unnatural – unusual in a pattern that is broadly in the Art Nouveau style.*

**687** *Different design elements are linked to create a tracery effect in this example of the popular 'fretting' or cut-out technique.*

*Europe and America*
# Art Nouveau 6

**688–689** *Two designs that derive from Eugène Grasset's study of botany and the way that plants develop so that each individual leaf and berry gets its fair share of the sun. Contemporary designers were interested in the notion of 'positive space' – the idea that the spaces around the forms are almost as interesting as the forms themselves.*

**690** *'Five-Leaved Ivy', a dense-field design created in 1897. Inspired by traditional Japanese art – especially by fabric printing – Eugène Grasset borrowed this motif from the sort of designs that, in Japan, would be appropriate in a woman's kimono worn in early summer or autumn.*

**691** *A dense and relatively naturalistic design, featuring horse chestnut flowers and leaves woven into a thick mat of line and colour.*

**692** *A detail from a wall frieze by R. Beauclair. The shape and form of this design bears witness to the fact that Beauclair drew inspiration from traditional Japanese motifs such as metal sword guards and clan and family crests, and from the paper stencils that were used to create printed cloth.*

**693** *The Art Nouveau style has sometimes been accused of being over-fussy and rather indulgent, but no one could object to the beautifully drawn, simplified curves of this lily-like flower.*

688

690

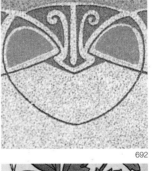
692

694

689

691

693

695

**694** *The iris, a motif commonly found in Japanese art, has different resonances in the West and the East. While to Western eyes it is a rather delicate and perhaps even feminine motif, in the context of Japanese art it was associated with samurai warriors. This design, entitled 'Iris', is from Eugène Grasset's* La plante et ses applications ornamentales, *published in 1897.*

**695** *The ever-popular iris motif again features in this design by Eugène Grasset, made about 1900. The design, with its strong linking lines, may well have been aimed at a stained-glass manufacturer. There was a huge popular interest in stained glass at this time, sparked off by the work of the American designer Louis Comfort Tiffany, who had recently introduced new colours and textures into the art of glassmaking.*

**696** *'Nasturtiums' is the title of this design — and on one level it is a fairly straightforward depiction of that subject. But on closer study, the viewer begins to see different influences emerging. The flower shapes, especially, are reminiscent of the uchiwa or round fan motifs that are seen in Japanese ukiyo-e woodblock prints.*

696

*Europe and America*
# Art Nouveau 7

**697** *Sinuous, organic-looking forms appear to engulf a symmetrical pattern of tulips and leaves in this late 19th-century printed cotton velvet from France. The English designer C. F. A. Voysey, who favoured a more restrained and lighter style, declared that designs such as this were not suited to the English climate and temperament.*

**698** *The black background to this printed cotton velvet shows off the curvaceous tulip forms to full effect. The 'whiplash' stems recall the famous Métro entrances in Paris designed by Hector Guimard. This fabric design was made about 1900 and printed a few years later by F. Steiner & Co.*

697

698

**699** *Autumn leaves and berries are rendered as flat areas of colour in this allover pattern. The design is thought to be by one of Grasset's colleagues or imitators.*

**700** *A detail from a printed fabric designed in 1898 by Samuel Rowe for Turnbull and Stockdale, a well-known fabric printer in Lancashire, England. The company sold their textiles to leading London stores such as Maples and Liberty's. This particular design sold very well, to the extent that the company asked the designer to revisit it and invent a series of patterns on the same theme. He eventually produced a dozen or so designs, using slightly different motifs and colours in each one, but sticking, more or less, to the same pattern.*

**701** *A detail from a printed cotton velvet, made by F. Steiner & Co. about 1906. In contrast to the realistic depiction of nature seen in **699**, the designer of this pattern has let his or her imagination run wild.*

**702** *Another traditional Japanese motif, the lily, features in this fabric from about 1889. The tendrils waving in the water, with their sinuous lines, were the ideal subject for an Art Nouveau designer.*

**703** *That recurrent Art Nouveau motif, the lily, is here combined with large stylised leaves, in vaguely heraldic shapes. This detail comes from a wall frieze design by J. Pfeiffer.*

**704** *A woven silk-and-wool cloth designed in 1900 by the Silver Studio for J. W. & C. Ward. The interesting thing about this design is the evident borrowings from William Morris – most visible in the way the leaves curl to show their undersides, and the organisation of the motifs on a vertical axis.*

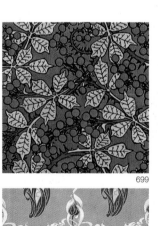
699

701

703

700

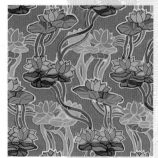
702

704

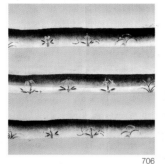

705

706

707

708

**705** *A detail from a 1920s design. Note the stylised flowers with part-arc centres all set against a ground of horizontal bands – all characteristic features of the Art Deco period.*

**706** *Delicate, freely drawn alpine flowers are arranged on broad bands of graduated yellow. This unusual design is from a fabric manufactured by the Wiener Werkstätte, the influential Vienna-based association of artist craftsmen.*

**707** *Stylised tulips and bell-like flowers jostle with each other for attention in this lively print. The design was created by Josef Hoffmann for the Wiener Werkstätte in 1911. Rather enigmatically, Hoffmann called the design 'Jagdfalke' ('Hunting Falcon').*

**708** *A detail from a 1930s English fabric design. By printing the single block of pattern on a staggered grid, interesting discords are created within the design.*

## *Europe, Asia and America*
# Early 20th Century

These patterns originate from a wide range of artists and influences including the Austrian and German design schools, European folk art, Japanese textile and graphic arts and Diaghilev's Ballets Russes, plus ideas from a number of contemporary art movements such as Cubism, Futurism and Constructivist art. Some can be termed 'Art Deco', even though this name stems from the 1925 International Exhibition in Paris that showed 'des Arts Décoratifs'. The motifs are mostly highly stylised versions of the ever-popular floral motifs or geometric abstractions of the newly built modernist buildings and machinery of the period. Designs in the form of enlarged details and strong lines, together with curving arabesques or energetic zigzags, are characteristic of the era and use chemical dyestuffs to achieve bold colour combinations.

*Europe, Asia and America*
# Early 20th Century 2

709

709 *A feast for the eyes, this abstract woven tapestry brings together an array of motifs and patterns, all united by the rich, reddish colour tones. It was created by Gunta Stolzl, head of the weaving workshop at the Bauhaus design school, Dessau, from 1927 to 1930.*

710 *An early 1930s design by the English designer John Churton of the Silver Studio. It draws its inspiration from the aggressive architectural forms of the period, especially those of French Cubism and Russian Constructivism.*

711 *'Ameise', a design by Eduard J. Wimmer-Wisgrill for a woven fabric for the Wiener Werkstätte Room in the Austrian Pavilion in Cologne, 1911. It was used for curtains and floor coverings. While the designer described the pattern as 'Neo-Biedermeier' – meaning belonging to the solid and conventional German style of the mid-19th century – the bamboo and flower motifs suggest that it was also influenced by Japanese art.*

712 *Two-colour printing lends a stencil-like appearance to this American fabric, which was*

designed by Orinoka Mills in 1929 for use in the Waldorf-Astoria Hotel in New York City. The gazelle motifs are based on a wrought-iron screen made by Edgar Brandt in 1925.

**713** A detail from a woven fabric, designed about 1932 by the Vereinigte Werkstätten cooperative, a group of textile artists in Munich. This particular pattern, entitled 'Venus' and featuring stylised tulips and flowers, was a characteristic Vereinigte design.

**714** Interesting optical effects are at play in this length of woven furnishing fabric, made in 1918 by William Foxton Ltd., London. Foxton based many of its fabrics on designs by famous artists of the period such as C. F. A. Voysey and L. C. Fraser.

**715** 'Roses with Red Thorns', a furnishing fabric made in England sometime between 1920 and 1930. Designs of this big, bold character – perfect for light furnishing and dress fabrics – were popular from the 1920s right through to the late 1940s.

710

713

711

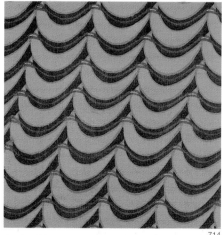

714

712

715

*Europe, Asia and America*
# Early 20th Century 3

**716** *A design by Charles Rennie Mackintosh, painted sometime between 1916 and 1923. This design, featuring a characteristic stylised flower and the signature gridded motif – the same motif that appeared on just about everything from architecture to furniture – is just one among many designs for fabrics produced by Mackintosh.*

716

718

720

717

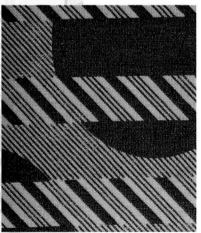

719

**717** *'Odette', a spray-painted fabric made in 1928 by Maria May, a painter and director of the Reiman School, Berlin. The spray technique involved covering areas of the cloth with a stencil and using an atomiser to spray liquid dye on to uncovered areas of the fabric.*

**718** *The starting point for this design was an interest in the way that the eye interprets as dynamic movement the counterchange between dark-on-light and light-on-dark. This screen-printed fabric was made in France in the 1920s.*

**719** *The 1920s and 1930s fashion for 'counterchange' design is evident in this printed cotton fabric,* produced in the United States about 1935. The juxtaposition of stripes of different widths creates a mesmerising optical illusion.

**720** With its undulating wave forms rendered in black line on a white background, this design draws its inspiration from Japanese woodblock printing. The detail is from a 1901 printed design by the graphic designer Koloman Moser. Two years later he co-founded the Wiener Werkstätte (with Josef Hoffmann), an association dedicated to what came to be called 'living art'.

**721** Detail from a spray-printed fabric entitled 'Lace', made in 1930 by Maria May. The angular forms are typical of the Deco style. May was inspired by Japanese and Indonesian textile printing techniques, especially batik.

**722** Rectilinear pattern, with a vertical emphasis, is combined with fluid, meandering line and the stylised profile of a woman's face. These elements are typical of the work of the Viennese 'Secession', a group of artists, led by Gustav Klimt, active around the turn of the century. This printed design was made in 1901 by Koloman Moser.

**723** A simple grid pattern forms the basis for a complex interplay of colours on this hand-woven tapestry or wall hanging. It was made in 1924 by Benita Koch-Otte at the famous Bauhaus school in Dessau.

**724** A printed textile by Josef Hoffmann, made in 1911. The flower motif within a grid recalls the designs of Charles Rennie Mackintosh, who was highly influential on Hoffmann's work.

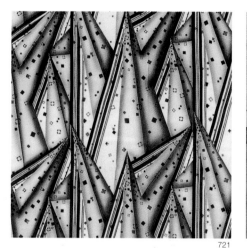

721

723

722

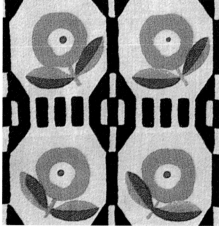

724

*Europe, Asia and America*
# Early 20th Century 4

725

726

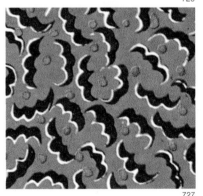

727

728

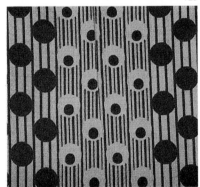

729

**725** *A detail from a woven upholstery fabric made by Erich Kleinhempel in 1924 for the Leipzig company Deutsche Textile Kunst. (Kleinhempel was the company's art director.) The somber tones and the way the motifs are edged with a stitch-like pattern are characteristic of Kleinhempel's work.*

**726** *The sketchy, informal drawing style gives this composition by Auguste H. Thomas a delightful freshness. It was first published in Thomas's book* Formes et couleurs *in the 1920s.*

**727** *Cloud-like forms float in a playful arrangement upon a sea-blue background. This detail comes from a printed fabric made in the United States in the late 1920s. Designs such as this were said to be in the 'French Mediterranean' style. The rounded cloud-like forms in the design were thought to give the pattern a cheerful, continental air, and the fresh colours added to the jolly effect.*

**728** *This design by G. Darcy was first published in* Or et couleurs *in 1920. The curious collection of seemingly unconnected imagery – seashells and leaves – and the way the images appear to be torn and pasted are all characteristics of Darcy's work.*

**729** *A detail from a printed fabric made in the United States in the late 1930s. The design stems in part from a popular interest in mechanisation and mass production. People realised that processes such as clenching rivets or punching holes in metal sheets could result in uniquely beautiful patterns.*

730

732

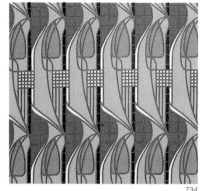

734

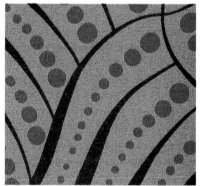

731

733

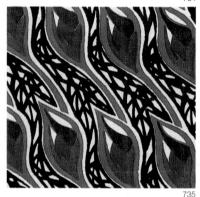

735

**730** *Produced by the Bauhaus textile studio in 1929, this wall hanging draws inspiration from African tribal textiles, especially strip cloths. It is woven in wool, on a cotton warp.*

**731** *A detail from a printed silk fabric made in the United States in the 1930s. The dot-and-furrow pattern can be linked to the development of micro-photography, which made it possible for the first time to see microscopic natural structures such as plant fibres.*

**732** *A hand-painted silk scarf made by Vereinigte Werkstätten in Munich, an association of several artists. The simple flower and leaf shapes floating on a grid of horizontal and vertical lines recall the paintings of the artist Paul Klee, but using a pale, watery palette.*

**733** *'Primitive' art from Africa and Oceania was popular in artistic circles in the 1920s. This cotton fabric shows the influence of African tribal art – both in terms of its simplified, angular forms and the block-printing technique used.*

**734** *The stylised flowers in a linear arrangement are typical of the work of Charles Rennie Mackintosh, while the gridded motif is one of his signatures. Mackintosh painted this textile design sometime between 1916 and 1923.*

**735** *Early 20th-century patterns run the whole gamut from naturalistic to completely abstract. Stylised leaf forms are combined with abstract motifs on this English furnishing fabric from about 1918, by William Foxton Ltd.*

## Europe, Asia and America
# Early 20th Century 5

**736** *Detail from a roller-printed cotton fabric, designed in England in 1921 for the Calico Printers Association, a group of print workers whose expressed aim was 'to preserve the traditions of the best of English calico printing'. The design was inspired by a late 19th-century Japanese print.*

**737** *An illustration, gouache on paper, by the artist Auguste H. Thomas for his book* Formes et couleurs, *published in Paris in the 1920s. The chrysanthemum and butterfly motifs, and their stencil-like appearance, draw inspiration from late 19th-century Japanese textiles and paper prints.*

**738** *The angular buildings in this textile design are similar to those seen on mass-produced English pottery of the 1920s and 1930s. The way the clouds are coloured to feather in from the edge is characteristic of the time. This detail is from a length of roller-printed cotton produced in England in 1928.*

**739** *Floral motifs are intersected by geometric shapes that cut across at different angles on this 1930s roller-printed fabric. The result is a shifting sense of perspective, similar to that seen in the work of French Cubist and Italian Futurist artists.*

**740** *'Wonderfully wild…brilliantly coloured and exotically primitive, just perfect'*

*is how one contemporary described the work of Minnie McLeish, who designed this roller-printed cotton fabric. It was made for William Foxton Ltd., London, in the 1920s. McLeish produced a number of similarly colourful designs.*

**741** *Made and sold in 1925 in the United States as 'French cotton', this block-printed cotton fabric was inspired by the large, richly coloured motifs that were being produced on the Continent, especially in France.*

**742** *Palm silhouettes and deep blue pools create an exotic mix in this fabric, called 'A Spanish Moon'. It was in fact designed in England in 1921.*

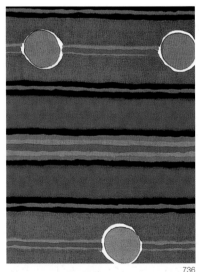

736

~738

740

737

739

741

*Europe, Asia and America*

# Early 20th Century 6

**743** *Designs with discordant vertical shapes were popular in the 1920s. This detail comes from a roller-printed fabric produced by Sanderson about 1921 as part of their 'Eton Rural' range. A reviewer described the design as having 'all the harmonious freedom and abandonment which is jazz'.*

**744** *Natural forms such as flowers, leaves and tendrils formed the starting point for this pen-and-ink design by*

743

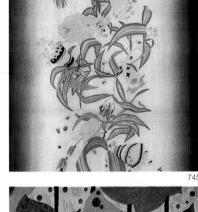

745

744

746

Charles Rennie Mackintosh. They are stylised almost to the point of abstraction, however, resulting in a strangely disturbing three-dimensional pattern. Mackintosh made this design in the 1920s, as he was moving away from design to devote himself primarily to watercolour painting.

**745** A riot of flowers and foliage cascades down this printed fabric, created at the Wiener Werkstätte in 1919 by

Dagobert Peche. Called 'Pan', the design is block-printed on a woven silk ground. The Werkstätte was the centre of progressive design in Vienna in the first part of the 20th century. Its designers and craftsmen aimed to combine aesthetic quality with utility.

**746** A detail from a block-printed cotton fabric created by the dress designer Paul Poiret in 1930. It was made for sale by Schumacher in the

United States, where Poiret's designs were popular. His personal signature was a stylised rose-like flower.

**747** This pattern of highly stylised oak leaves drew inspiration from the sets and costumes of Diaghilev's Ballets Russes. The gouache-on-paper design featured in Auguste H. Thomas's pattern book Formes et couleurs.

**748** Archaeological discoveries in Egypt in the 1920s fired the popular imagination and for a while the fashion world seemed to go Nile crazy. Palms, pharaohs and pyramids were everywhere. This frieze-like detail from a printed cotton fabric made in France in the late 1920s shows a small section from 'King Tut's' throne.

**749** Big and bright, with bold slashes of colour, this design is typical of the work of Scottish designer Minnie McLeish. Its colour combinations are reminiscent of the work of Fauve artists such as Matisse and Derain. The roller-printed cotton furnishing fabric was made for William Foxton Ltd., London, about 1925.

**750** A detail from a fabric made in the United States in the 1930s. Around this time there was great interest in new scientific discoveries surrounding the movement of fluids and gases. This artist may well have drawn inspiration from diagrams in a scientific journal.

749

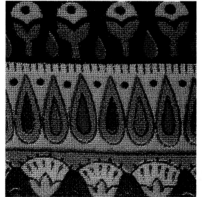
748

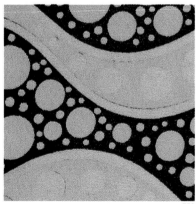
750

*Europe, Asia and America*
# Early 20th Century 7

**754** *The light-hearted playfulness of Art Deco is perfectly captured by this summery design of stylised flowers, created in 1929 by A. Erdmann. A contemporary reviewer said:'It reminds us more of our wishes, hopes, joys, more of holidays, summer and peaceful rest than of reality with its ideological dictates, its world of work and its political power plays. This fabric wants to be more cheerful than reality would permit'.*

**751** *Dazzling colour combinations are used in this pattern of stylised roses, inspired by the work of Leon Bakst and others for Diaghilev's Ballets Russes. The design was published in Thomas's Formes et couleurs.*

**752** *A block-printed design on a cotton fabric, shown at the textile exhibition Moderne Bildwirkereien in Dessau, Germany, in 1929. The chevron motifs and two-tone 'cut-out' shapes are characteristic of the Art Deco style.*

**753** *The motifs seen here – tendrils, bell flowers, leaves and stems – are similar to those used by Art Nouveau artists. The treatment, however, with bold blocks of colour, is more modern. This sample for a printed cotton fabric by Lotte Fromel-Fochler was made about 1911 and is taken from a Wiener Werkstätte pattern book. The artist had probably seen similar large, open patterns when the Ballets Russes toured Austria.*

753

751

752

754

**757** *Colourful crocuses on a vibrant blue background evoke a feeling of joy and springtime. Fabrics such as this were a breath of fresh air to a generation brought up on the heavy patterns of the Victorian parlour. Like* **756***, left, this roller-printed cotton was produced by Sanderson as part of the 'Eton Rural' range. Designed in the 1920s, it went in and out of production right through to the early 1950s.*

**755** *Japanese forms often gave Charles Rennie Mackintosh a starting point for his designs. Here he draws inspiration from a whole range of Japanese motifs – chrysanthemums, irises, peonies and perhaps even the Japanese umbrella – to create an exciting allover pattern. Mackintosh probably made this pen-and-ink design in the late 1920s. It is certainly very different from his earlier style, which is characterised by its restrained line and stylised forms.*

**756** *A detail from a roller-printed fabric produced by the English wallpaper and textile manufacturers Arthur Sanderson and Son about 1921. Sanderson was established in 1860 and went on to become one of Britain's biggest textile companies. Variations on this tulip-and-narcissus design were produced after the war using brighter colours on new man-made fabrics. The design remained popular right through to the end of the 1950s.*

755

756

757

*Europe, Asia and America*
# Early 20th Century 8

**758** *Stylised flowers are strewn across a dark background, which emphasises the sumptuous colouring of the blooms. This design was produced about 1912 by Reni Schaschl-Schuster for the Wiener Werkstätte. Schaschl-Schuster favoured delicate, floral designs. In addition to textiles she designed ceramics, glass and graphics.*

**759** *This intricate, eye-dazzling pattern is made up of interlocking geometric shapes that appear to float above the blue and red stripes behind. The motifs draw inspiration from Japanese graphics and embroidery. The design was produced about 1912 by Lotte Fromel-Fochler, for the Wiener Werkstätte. Fromel-Fochler was an influential*

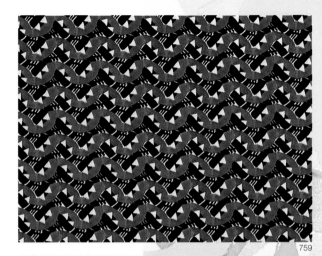

759

760

758

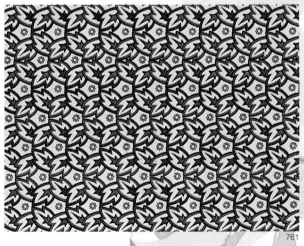

761

762

763

764

member of the artists' association who specialised in textiles, printing, lace and embroidery.

**760** *Tiny stylised birds are arranged within a strict grid on this fabric, produced about 1912 for the Wiener Werkstätte. While the artist is unknown, the layout suggests that it could be by Lotte Fromel-Fochler.*

**761** *A textile design by Fritzi Low-Lazar, produced in the early 1920s for the Wiener Werkstätte. This design is typical of her work, in that it uses stylised natural forms, leaves and flowers to produce motifs that are characterised by their strong and jagged appearance.*

**762** *Abstract forms appear to dance across the surface of this pattern, lending it a dynamic feeling of movement. The vigorous, angular forms and overall 'jazzy' feel are very much in the Art Deco style. This textile design comes from a printed linen sample book by Karl Krenek, produced in the 1920s for the Wiener Werkstätte. While Krenek was primarily a painter, graphic artist and designer of ceramics, he also supplied the Wiener Werkstätte with a number of textile designs such as this.*

**763** *Based on a system of interlocking blocks, this textile design features a variety of motifs and techniques in a carefully composed and balanced order. The delicate drawing style, the cross-hatching, the 'star' motif and even the muted green and yellow colours all anticipate textile designs of the 1950s; see, for example, patterns* **839–840** *(pages 274–275) and* **851** *(page 277). The design is by Josef Hoffmann, co-founder of the Wiener Werkstätte, who was instrumental in the general move towards artistic abstraction in the decorative arts during the early 20th century.*

**764** *A detail from a printed textile by Mitzi Friedmann-Otten, a Wiener Werkstätte artist who designed metalwork, jewellery, and enamels, as well as textiles. Friedmann-Otten was one of the prime movers of the Wiener Werkstätte style, especially in the years following World War I. While the starting point of this pattern was a collection of open envelopes spread out on a desk, the structure of the design draws inspiration from the stylised abstracted forms seen in Cubist, Futurist and Constructivist art.*

*Europe, Asia and America*
# Early 20th Century 9

765

766

768

767

769

**765** *A design, gouache on paper, by the Russian Constructivist artist Varvara Stepanova, 1924. The Constructivists advocated machine production, industrial materials and abstract forms. The motif in this design is based on the propeller-style fans once common in factories and workshops.*

**766** *A detail from an artist's illustration, gouache on paper, painted in the 1920s by Auguste H. Thomas for his book* Formes et couleurs. *The stylised chrysanthemum motif draws inspiration from oriental prints.*

**767** *The candy colours and 'target' motifs on this pattern are strikingly similar to the Pop Art prints of the 1960s (for example, see patterns* **949** *and* **950** *on page 302). In fact, this silk fabric created by the French artist E. A. Séguy was shown in 1925 at the Paris International Exhibition of Decorative Arts.*

**768** *Plant forms provided the starting point for this 1918 textile design by Carl Otto Czeshka, called 'Mode Herbst' ('Autumn Fashion'). The design featured in a Wiener Werkstätte sample book. Czeshka's work ranged from calendars and theatre design through to jewellery, metalwork and of course textiles.*

**769** *The elegant, light-footed gazelle was a favourite Art Deco motif (see also pattern* **712** *on page 241). This detail comes from a 1930 printed cotton textile by Paul Poiret for F. Schumacher & Co. Poiret was one of the early 20th century's most innovative fashion designers.*

**770** *The early 20th century's fascination with the exotic and the 'primitive' is illustrated by this gouache-on-paper design, which is packed with fascinating detail. Called 'Primeval Forest', it was designed in Austria by Ludwig Heinrich Jungernickel in 1913.*

*Europe, Asia and America*
# Early 20th Century 10

**771** *Fronds and foliage were the original inspiration for this flowing, painterly design made by Dagobert Peche in 1912. Peche was one of the leading members of the Wiener Werkstätte and ran the Zurich branch from 1917 to 1919. His style, however, was very different from the geometric manner of Werkstätte co-founder Josef Hoffmann.*

**772** *Smooth arcs and disk forms are mixed with straight lines and sharp angles in this boldly coloured design. It comes from the 1920s pattern book* Kaleidoscope: ornements abstraits *by M. P. Verneuil. The jutting shapes look forward to the jagged modernism of Art Deco.*

**773** *Loosely based on a leaf pattern, this illustration by G. Darcy comes from the pattern book* Or et couleurs *published in Paris in 1920.*

**774** *Look carefully at this design and you will see that it is a play on the traditional Japanese carp motif. The overall design was inspired by Japanese stencil printing. The artist was Koloman Moser, co-founder of the Wiener Werkstätte.*

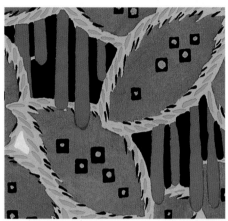

773

771

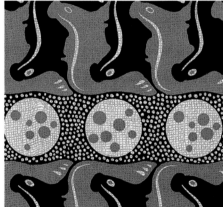

774

772

775

776

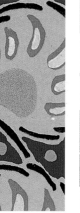

777

778

779

**775** *This striking graphic pattern is by the Japanese artist Yoshinosuke, and was included in a collection published in 1928. The bold shapes and earthy palette are reminiscent of African tribal art, which was itself particularly fashionable in the late 1920s.*

**776** *A design by a member of the Omega Workshops, London, printed about 1913. The workshops were set up by the artist Roger Fry to apply the talents of artists to the design of household items such as furniture, textiles and pottery. This pattern, 'Amenophis', was inspired in part by the Egyptian pharaoh Amenhotep III, who erected many of Egypt's most famous buildings.*

**777** *An artist's illustration painted in the 1920s by G. Darcy for his book Or et couleurs. The stylised flower, possibly a chrysanthemum, recalls traditional Japanese textiles and paper prints.*

**778** *A popular interest in paper-cuts and collage probably inspired the idea for this fabric design from the 1920s. A number of artists were experimenting with cut-paper techniques at this time.*

**779** *Two popular Eastern motifs – the rolling wave and the falling leaf – form the basis for this design by Koloman Moser. It was eventually produced as a wall covering, a printed cotton fabric and a heavy woven upholstery textile.*

*Europe, Asia and America*

# Early 20th Century 11

**780** *This spray-printed textile combines a number of Parisian-inspired motifs including the Eiffel Tower, dancers, and a café. Unsurprisingly called 'Paris', it was created by Maria May in 1929–30 while she was senior instructor at the Schule Reimann in Berlin. The illustrative style is a forerunner of many 1950s patterns.*

**781** *A variety of fish and underwater flora make up this enchanting fabric print from 1928 – a joint effort by Victor von Rauch and Wilhelm Marsmann. Together they founded the Deutsche Farbmobel AG Munich, which specialised in the production of artistic utility items, mainly textiles.*

**782** *A detail from a 1922 textile design by the English painter and designer George Sherringham, made for Seftons and Co. Sherringham drew inspiration from various natural forms, among them flowers, cross-sectioned fruit and seashells.*

**783** *An unusual pattern design that apparently sets out to create the illusion of a heavily textured woven fabric. The gouache-on-paper design was produced in France sometime in the 1920s, by an unknown artist.*

**784** *Boldly drawn flowers sit upon a background of regular black and white stripes. This textile design by Gustav Kalhammer was made about 1911*

780

781

782

for the Wiener Werkstätte. Kalhammer was very interested in plants and in folk art. His patterns tend to feature crisp and stylised plant forms on a geometrical grid, with images often inspired by traditional motifs.

**785** 'Blue Roses', a detail from a textile design created in 1922 by the artist designer Percy Bilbie for F.W. Grafton and Co. The rose motif and the grid format clearly pay homage to Charles Rennie Mackintosh. However, the striking colours – blue roses on a vibrant yellow background – and underlying geometrical pattern mark this out as more than a mere copy of the famous Scottish artist's work.

**786** A detail from a textile design made in 1923 by Josef Hoffmann, co-founder of the Wiener Werkstätte. This design, with its neat lozenges and circles all set in a geometrical grid, is a reworking of an earlier pattern produced in 1915.

784

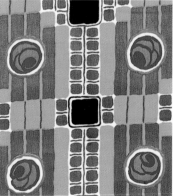

785

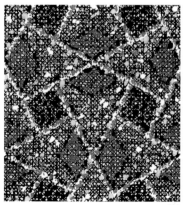

783

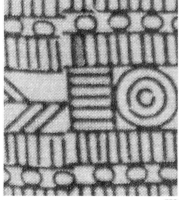

786

*Europe, Asia and America*
# Early 20th Century 12

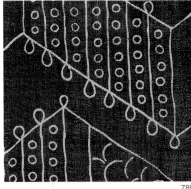

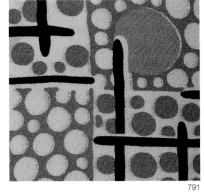

787

789

791

788

790

792

**787** *The spacing of the horizontal bars within this pattern indicates that it was inspired by tapestry-woven 'counterchange' designs. The detail comes from a printed cotton fabric, produced in France about 1925.*

**788** *An illustration painted in the 1920s by Auguste H. Thomas for his book* Formes et couleurs. *As with a*

*great many of his patterns, the primary motifs – the stylised flowers – and the way that they are arranged draw inspiration from traditional Japanese art.*

**789** *A French printed cotton from the 1920s. During this period many designers were fascinated by tribal art and liked to build 'ethnic' details and motifs into their designs. The detailing*

*within this design was inspired by the dot-dash-and-zigzag sequences seen on some Oceanic barkcloths.*

**790** *A detail from a printed fabric, made in 1912 by Dagobert Peche for the Wiener Werkstätte. Both the black-and-white printing and the motifs themselves are adapted from traditional Japanese stencil prints.*

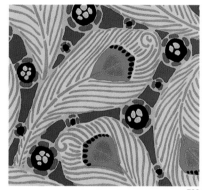
793

795

794

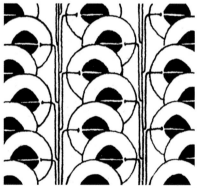
796

**793** *Peacock feathers, a favourite of Eastern artists, are reduced to their bare essentials in this artist's illustration. The design reflects the interest in 'exotic' motifs that was prevalent in the 1920s.*

**794** *The stylised closed rose was Charles Rennie Mackintosh's favourite motif, and he used it throughout his career. In this pen-and-ink textile design, created sometime in the late 1920s, Mackintosh has packed the roses close together upon a characteristic checkerboard grid.*

**795** *A detail from a block-printed cotton fabric – designer unknown – made in the United States sometime in the late 1920s or early 1930s. Although the peach motif is borrowed from Eastern patterns, the bold colours and the crisp naive shapes in this design are strikingly similar to patterns seen on early American painted furniture and quilts.*

**791** *There is a faintly scientific air to this textile, which was made in the United States in the late 1930s. At this time there was great interest in mechanisation and mass production. When artists and designers saw mechanised processes in action, they were keen to adapt these modern developments in terms of pattern-making.*

**792** *In yet another debt to Japanese art, the stylised fruit and feathery leaves in this design look as if they have been dashed off with a brush. This gouache-on-paper illustration was painted in the 1920s by G. Darcy.*

**796** *A detail of an outline design, called 'Baumfalke', by Koloman Moser. First produced in 1911, this design draws inspiration from the formal broken circles of Japanese patterns. In the final design, the outer rings of the stylised flowers were to be coloured a rich blue.*

*Europe, Asia and America*
# Early 20th Century 13

in 1924 by Ernst Aufseeser. A professor at Düsseldorf from 1919 until 1933, Aufseeser designed fabrics, wallpapers, graphics and ceramics. He designed for various artists' workshops and for Deutsche Textil Kunst in Leipzig.

**797** *A detail from a French roller-printed fabric, made about 1928, designer unknown. The bisected circle or dot is known as a split-pea or screw. A feeling of movement has been achieved by varying the direction of the slot.*

**798** *Felix Rix made this Japanese-influenced, block-printed design, 'Poppies', for the Wiener Werkstätte in 1929. Rix was so interested in Japanese art that he moved to Kyoto in 1935. He held a professorship at the Municipal Academy of Art there from 1949 to 1963.*

**799** *Designed by Pablo Picasso, this woven cotton-and-linen fabric was made by the manufacturer Rodier for the famous interior designer Jean-Michel Frank. The circles and stepped squares are characteristic Picasso motifs from his Cubist period.*

**800** *At first glance this exquisite design of broad stripes with delicate vases of flowers seems not too far removed from certain 18th-century, classically inspired patterns. The fish, however, are a curious addition. This hand-printed fabric was designed*

799

797

798

800

**801** *Subtle gradations in tone, typical of the Art Deco style, give this two-colour design an illusion of depth, despite the flatness of the motifs. This upholstery fabric was designed in 1928 by E. Engelbrechet for the Vereinigte Werkstätten in Munich. The firm specialised in producing woven furnishings of a very high quality for luxury liners – including entire rooms and interior design settings for the liner Bremen in 1929.*

**802** *A detail from a printed fabric, designed in 1930 by Josef Hillerbrand, for Deutsche Werkstätten in Dresden. Hillerbrand's designs of this period are characterised by their 'open' quality, with motifs arranged on an underlying grid of dots. He did freelance work for Deutsche Werkstätten and eventually became one of the institution's most important contributors, designing printed fabrics, carpets, wallpapers, ceramics, glass and furniture.*

**803** *Rigorously disciplined, this rectilinear-patterned tapestry was woven by Anni Albers in 1926 at the Bauhaus. The design school's ideal that form should follow function declared that textile patterns should be the result of the weaving technique, rather than being printed, which ignored the underlying weave. Anni was married to the painter and Bauhaus teacher Josef Albers, and the work of both artists is characterised by a rational approach.*

801

802

803

*Europe, Asia and America*
# Early 20th Century 14

804 With its horizontal stripes of different tones and textures, this design draws inspiration from African tribal strip-cloth weaving. The detail comes from an upholstery fabric by Sigmund von Weech, woven in 1929 for his Hand Weaving Studio in Schaftlach. Von Weech designed fabrics and curtains, and became the director of the Höhere Fachschule für Textil Bekleidungsindustrie in Berlin in 1931.

805 Blocks of pattern and colour are carefully planned to create a logical, measured design that is also aesthetically pleasing. This woven cover by Ruth Hollos-Consemuller was made at the Bauhaus in 1927, and displays the artistic integrity demanded by the design school's teaching.

806 The 'fragmented' look of this pattern owes much to contemporary artistic experiments with shifting perspective and points of view. This roller-printed cotton fabric was made by W. Foxton Ltd., London, in 1929.

804

**807** *The floral designs produced by the English firm Sanderson & Son were enormously popular during the early 20th century. This print dates from the 1920s.*

**808** *Franco-Russian abstract art provided the inspiration for this woven fabric sample. It was made by Sonia Delaunay for the Wiener Werkstätte in 1925.*

**809** *The stylised bird and plant motifs seen here are typical of the work of Josef Hillerbrand, who designed this printed fabric in 1929. Hillerbrand was one of the leading artists of the Deutsche Werkstätten in Dresden, contributing designs for fabrics and carpets.*

**810** *A detail from a woven fabric produced in 1925. Its heavy, dark quality, and the stylised rose and acorn motifs, suggests that the artist drew inspiration from medieval designs and possibly from late 19th-century English designers such as William Morris.*

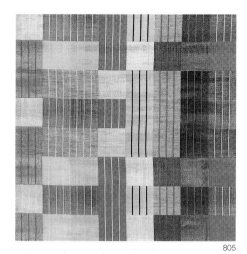

805

808

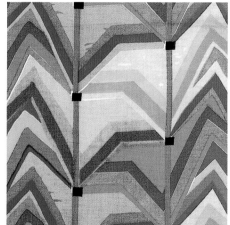

806

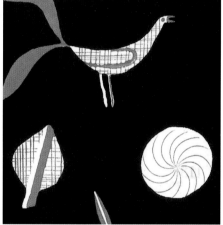

809

807

810

*Europe, Asia and America*
# Early 20th Century 15

**811** *The furthest reaches of the Soviet empire are celebrated in this 1930s cotton print, entitled 'Turkestan Siberia Railway'. From the late 1920s onwards, Soviet design became strongly propagandist. Constructivist experiments with abstraction were no longer encouraged.*

**812** *This intricately detailed cotton print is a joyous celebration of Russian folk art. It was made in the late 1920s by S. Burylin, after a design by the artist Bilibin. It goes somewhat against the mood of the times, which wanted to break with the past.*

**813** *A detail from a Russian printed cotton made in the early 1930s. The vaguely explosive motif linked by sharply angled lines and the vivid, sharply contrasting colours ally this fabric to the notion that the power of science would create a brave new world–one which would need 'brave' new patterns to match.*

**814** *Post-revolutionary Russian artists were strongly encouraged to produce designs based on the 'innate beauty of function and industrialisation'. Themes such as construction, factories and transport were all favoured. 'Soviet Aviation', a 1932 cotton print, glorifies the achievements of the new age.*

**815** *While promoting newly mechanised agriculture, in accordance with Soviet dictates, this print also experiments with optical effects and geometric forms in the Constructivist manner. The fabric was designed by S. Burylin in 1930.*

**816** *First shown in 1925 at the Paris International Exhibition of Decorative Arts, this sateen fabric features the emblems of the Soviet Union: sickle, hammer and ears of wheat, all set against a rising sun. The final impression, ironically, recalls the bold American designs seen in comics of the 1950s. The designer was the Russian O. Gruin.*

811

812

813

814

815

817

# 1940s & 1950s

**817** *Detail from a fabric design produced in England in the late 1950s. The design, in sharp, clear sections, draws inspiration from the new flexible, plastic materials of the time.*

**818** *The world of science and technology inspired this early 1950s pattern. The intriguing motifs are based around molecular structures and scientific instruments.*

**819** *'Wigwam', a screen-printed fabric designed by Mary Duncan in 1947 for Cresta Silk Ltd. At first glance the pattern appears abstract, but if you look carefully you can see the imagery of Hollywood Westerns: wigwams, cacti and Native American symbols.*

**820** *The polka dot was hugely popular in the 1950s and featured on everything from clothing and accessories to adhesive decals. This fabric is in one of the classic polka-dot combinations: white dots on a red background.*

818

819

820

These patterns are mostly examples of mass-produced 'modern' or 'good' designs produced by designers working in Europe and America at this time. They often portray whimsical asymmetrical shapes that are freely drawn and based on the contemporary preoccupations of speed, space travel, technology, the depiction of molecular structures and new inventions such as the television. These are frequently represented by curving, spinning motifs that seem to float in a space filled with mysterious clouds. Other common elements are patterns with an emphasis on vertical lines combined with large leaf forms or stylised flowers. These patterns were often depicted in a highly unnatural palette of colours such as acid greens and reds or muddy browns. Another preoccupation is the romantic portrayal of the Wild West.

*Europe and America*
# 1940s & 1950s 2

**821** 'Mobile', a screen-printed rayon fabric designed by June Lyon in 1954 for Heals in London. The design draws its inspiration from the mobiles and other wire-suspended structures made by the American sculptor Alexander Calder. Calder's influence permeated 1950s design, from textiles and graphics to furniture and fittings.

**822** Autumn leaves, in earthy hues, are arranged in a dynamic pattern – they almost look as if they are falling – on a dark background. This late 1940s or early 1950s English roller-printed fabric is in many ways an updated version of a classic William Morris design.

**823** The thick black outlines of these big, bold floral motifs recall the imagery of science-fiction comics. This American printed design dates from the late 1940s.

**824** A detail from a woven cotton fabric made in America in the mid-1950s. While the colours have been warmed up and arranged to suit the vibrant imagery of the period –

lots of extruded plastics and widths of rayon – the designer's starting point was Edwardian canvas awnings, the sort of drapes that were hung over doors and porches.

**825** A detail from a roller-printed fabric design, made in the late 1940s or early 1950s. Contemporary TV imagery inspired the fast-moving wheel pattern – a mix of automobiles and Wild West wagons.

**826** The wonders of science and technology inspired this design, which is based on the molecular structure of haemoglobin. These are the kinds of patterns and forms that you can expect to see when you look through a microscope. This sample of woven silk was designed in England in 1951, by Bernard Rowland for the Festival Pattern Group.

**827** Modern technology was the starting point for this 1940s or 1950s design. The motifs call to mind high-rise buildings, electrical wiring circuits and conveyor-belt delivery.

**828** This light-hearted and quirky English printed cotton, 'Coupons', dates from the 1940s when British wartime clothes rationing was finally coming to an end. The sketchy illustrative style is a forerunner of the 1950s style.

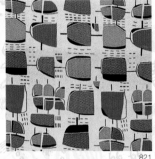
821

824

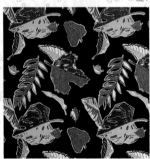
822

825

823

826

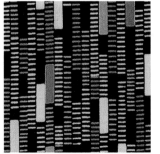
827

*Europe and America*

# 1940s & 1950s 3

**829** *A printed nursery fabric, probably American, designed in the early 1950s. The images come from cowboy comics and TV programmes: note the ranch complete with well and stock fencing.*

**830** *A detail from a printed playroom fabric, produced in the early 1950s. Inspired by the popularity of circus movies and comics, big-top animals and clowns feature together in a cheery melee.*

**831** *While this printed cotton sample, made in the mid 1950s, taps into the Wild West craze, it also draws inspiration from 19th-century American folk art — paintings and patchworks — where designs were shown 'flat on', in the naive or primitive style.*

**832** *The movie* Davy Crockett and the River Pirates *inspired this American cotton fabric. Crockett mania gripped the nation in the 1950s, when this print was made.*

**833** *A Wild West craze swept through America and Europe in the 1950s, and every child wanted a cowboy outfit complete with a holster and six-shooter. This detail comes from a 1950s pattern book.*

829

832

830

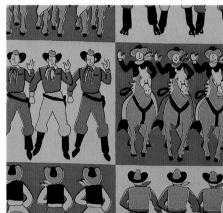

833

831

834

835

836

837

**834** *1950s children could live in a cowboy's world, watching Wild West movies on TV, then retire to themed bedrooms with cowboy paper, fabric and accessories to match. This cotton fabric, featuring cowboys, steers and cacti, was made in England in the mid-1950s.*

**835** *Detail from a printed cotton, produced in the mid-1950s and probably American. Although this design does draw inspiration from the West, it avoids the more obvious Stetson-and-boots imagery, instead showing comparatively realistic New Mexican scenes.*

**836** *While this printed cotton sample was undoubtedly produced in the 1950s it harks back to the mid-1940s, when some designers were keen to experiment with ways of 'modernising' traditional floral prints. The leaf-like motif also suggests human lips.*

**837** *A detail from a pattern for paper and fabric, made in America in the early 1950s. Every child in the 1950s wanted a cowboy outfit, but perhaps the next best thing was to have wallpaper featuring cowboy boots, ten-gallon hats, cacti and sheriff's badges.*

*Europe and America*
# 1940s &
# 1950s 4

**838** *The flat, stencil-like shapes and vibrant mix of oranges and blues are typical of the work of Duncan Grant, who designed this screen-printed cotton velvet for Allan Walton Textiles in London. Grant was a renowned painter who had previously worked for the Omega Workshops (see* **776**, *page 257).*

**839** *The TV-screen motif and the 'ball-and-rod' structure seen here (described variously as 'splitting the atom', 'atomic swizzle stick' and 'cocktail cherry on a stick') were ubiquitous in the 1950s. They can be seen in everything from clock faces and textiles to lamps, furniture and cutlery. This English curtain fabric dates from the mid-1950s.*

**840** *The leaf-like forms, spindly stars and abstract, seemingly hand-cut shapes are all typical of 1950s design. Similar motifs can be found on 1950s furniture, sculpture and ceramics. Patterns such as this were marketed as 'contemporary' and 'organic'. This detail comes from a curtain fabric.*

**841** *A roller-printed curtain fabric, probably English, made in the 1950s. While this design was inspired by the craze for Wild West imagery – cowboys and Indians, bucking broncos and mountains – it also links up with the craze for the circus with its stunt riders and performers. This would have been a choice curtain material for a boy's room in the 1950s.*

838

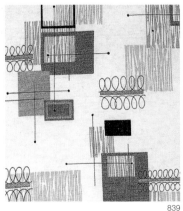

839

842 *Whirling shapes appear to float in space on this printed cotton fabric, made in England in the late 1950s. Motifs such as this were highly popular at the time. Unidentified flying objects and the space race had gripped the public imagination, especially following the Soviet Union's launch of the Sputnik satellite in 1957.*

843 *A detail from a curtain fabric, designed by the English artist John Piper in 1955, produced by David Whitehead Ltd. The motifs are based on ornaments found on the roofs of English medieval buildings.*

844 *A detail from a sample of roller-printed cotton by the American designer Rockwell Kent, made in 1950. The dove symbolises peace, the wheat sheaf symbolises abundance and the peaceful town with its church and barns is a celebration of peace and prosperity and of all things American.*

842

843

841

844

840

*Europe and America*
# 1940s &
# 1950s 5

**845** *A detail from a screen-printed fabric designed in Sweden in 1952 by Stig Lindberg. The design, entitled 'Apples', takes its inspiration from traditional 18th- and 19th-century Swedish tapestries. The simplified drawing style is very 1950s, however. If you look closely at the different apple motifs you will see that the whole life cycle is illustrated, from seed to decomposition.*

**846** *While the form of this pattern simulates ethnic block prints, the rippled offset character of the motifs is inspired by abstract art. The detail comes from a late 1940s printed textile.*

845

846

**847** *Aerial photographs showing the shattered grid of a city after an atomic explosion are thought to have been the original inspiration for this style of pattern, popular in the late 1950s. Fear of the atomic bomb was transmuted into all kinds of 'warning' patterns and motifs, but the designs weren't properly 'read' until 20 years later.*

**848** *A detail from an American screen-printed fabric, made for a child's room in the 1950s. The galloping cowboy motif was inspired by Wild West comics, movies and TV shows.*

**849** *In the 1950s, the sports car became a symbol of the new go-faster, got-to-have-it-now lifestyle, an image of success and sophistication. This fabric was made in England in the 1950s and vividly depicts an appealing variety of sporty models that would have been desirable – and, for most, unattainable – at the time.*

**850** *A printed textile, designed in England in the late 1950s. The design is entitled 'Mobiles', suggesting that the individual motifs were inspired by the twisting, colourful shapes of the mobiles that were part of contemporary interior decor. Soft, rounded corners on square shapes were a consistent feature of 1950s patterns. Motifs of*

*this type were often printed on plastic fabrics used to cover the chairs, banquettes and work surfaces of the newly fashionable breakfast nooks that featured in many a stylish kitchen-diner.*

**851** *A detail from an American printed fabric made in the early 1950s. The design brings together the 'cocktail cherry on a stick' or 'atomic swizzle stick' motif (see pattern* **839**, *page 274) – one of the most widely used forms of the period – and delicately drawn, abstracted geometric shapes to create what can be instantly recognised as a classic 1950s pattern.*

849

847

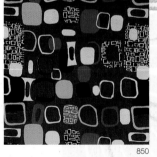
850

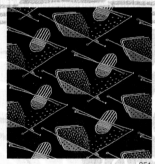
851

848

*Europe and America*
# 1940s & 1950s 6

852

853

855 *A late 1940s American design that shows the mixed influences of its time: the mobiles of Alexander Calder, the sculptures of Barbara Hepworth, the paintings of Joan Miró and the widespread use of wire and tubular steel in product design.*

855

854

856

852 *A printed fabric from a 1950s sample book. The design brings together the vertical strip and the overblown, tropical leaf to create a pattern characteristic of the decade.*

853 *A pattern for an American 1950s tie. The craze for brightly coloured ties at this time, combined with the fact that there didn't need to be repeat*

*within the design, gave the designer a perfect opportunity to allow his or her imagination run free.*

854 *The boomerangs on this 1950s French fabric were probably inspired by modern sculpture. The 'organic' forms made by sculptor Barbara Hepworth were especially influential, as were the cup-shaped Charles Eames's chairs.*

856 *With its painterly brush strokes and swirls, this abstract pattern was designed to imitate the work of famous contemporary artists. The detail comes from a printed cotton fabric made in France in the late 1950s.*

857 *The images on this textile – the artist's palette and brushes, the Eiffel Tower in Paris, the Colosseum in*

857

859

**861** *'Web', a screen-printed textile design by the celebrated English artist Graham Sutherland. The harsh, angular lines are typical of his style. Sutherland thought of his textile designs as a way of bringing his art closer to the public.*

861

858

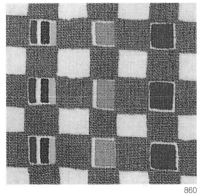

860

862

Rome, windmills in Holland — are intended to convey an air of sophistication. Probably English, it was designed in the 1950s.

**858** *A 1950s fabric, probably French. Stylised savannah was a popular theme, in large part a response to the huge interest in nature and wildlife programmes on TV and at the cinema.*

**859** *A detail from a 1950s English roller-printed cotton. The motifs are formed from bold areas of flat colour in typical 1950s colours: dusky green-blue, pale yellow, red and grey.*

**860** *This late 1940s printed fabric is inspired by expensive woven fabrics and by the interest in geometric forms seen in contemporary architecture.*

**862** *A screen-printed textile design, artist unknown, made in England in the 1950s. The design draws inspiration from Japanese printing in the black outlines of the drawing, in the way the fruit motifs relate one to another, and in the delicate interplay between the motifs and the space around them.*

*Europe and America*
# 1940s & 1950s 7

**863** *A detail from a 1950s English printed textile. The theme of falling autumn leaves was very popular, especially when the leaves were arranged between broad vertical stripes. In many ways this design harks back to late 19th-century William Morris patterns.*

**864** *A design from an American 1950s tie. The craze for colourful ties with huge patterns led to unique pieces being marketed as 'individual works of art'.*

**865** *This screen-printed textile taps into the popular interest in art, architecture and furniture design. The pattern features swiftly drawn design doodles as might be seen in an architect's or designer's sketchbook.*

**866** *A pattern of bottles, bowls and goblets somehow evokes the idea of a sophisticated*

*and bohemian lifestyle. This 1950s English textile dates from a time when people wanted to put wartime austerity behind them and look forward to a brighter, more light-hearted future.*

**867** *'Fugue', a textile designed by the English artist Paul Nash. Although this design was created in the late 1930s it was reprinted several times during the 1950s, and the abstracted anthropomorphic figures appear to be very much of that era.*

**868** *This textile design is related to contemporary interest in artists, sculpture and artists' models. It playfully refers to the styles of Henry Moore, Barbara Hepworth and Alberto Giacometti, all of whom had a high profile in the 1950s.*

**869** *Classical Greek sculpture was the inspiration for this screen-printed design by the artist Duncan Grant. The patches of flat colour and the sweeping, sketchy lines can be found in many 1950s patterns.*

863

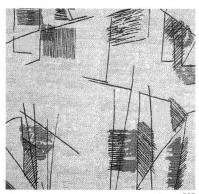

865

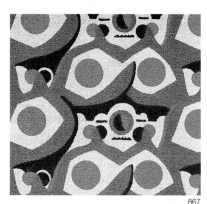

867

864

866

868

869

*Europe and America*
# 1940s &
# 1950s 8

**870** *The characteristic 1930s combination of stepped geometric forms and stylised naturalistic motifs found new expression in the 1950s, and designs like this can be found on many wallpapers and fabrics of the period.*

**871** *The sketchily drawn double lines around the main motifs in this pattern make the images appear to move and shimmer. This 1950s design may have been influenced by the popular craft pastime of making plaster casts of leaves.*

**872** *A detail from a 1950s printed textile that, while updating and imitating the* block-and-lino-printed designs of the 1930s and 1940s, also recalls the strong contemporary interest in 'primitive' art. The way in which the motifs are printed as blocks suggests that the artist was inspired by African tribal printing and Indonesian batiks.

**873** *A detail from a screen-printed cotton fabric made in the 1950s in England. With its quirky figures and naive style the design recalls the work of the Russian-born artist Marc Chagall, who worked in Paris in the 1920s and 1930s. Chagall's paintings illustrate fragments of memories, his village and family.*

870

875

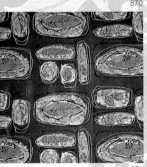

871

873

874

**874** *An assortment of seemingly unrelated motifs float on a red background in this printed design. The bricks may be a reference to the wave of new home building that took place in the 1950s, while the squiggly lines could relate to the fashion for bent wire furniture and other items. The 'cut-out' look and bold colour contrasts recall the work of the French artist Henri Matisse.*

**875** *The sweeping diagonal lines of this pattern — and the way the angular motifs seem to swirl and clash against each other — give it a dynamic quality. Although abstract it somehow evokes the interests of the period — fast cars, flight, space travel and science. The detail comes from an early 1950s English textile.*

**876** *Not all 1950s patterns looked to the future. This English textile builds on motifs found in traditional Indian textiles, cashmere shawls and carpets: the realistic flower and the ancient boteh motif. The teardrop-shaped boteh traditionally represents long life and fertility.*

876

*Europe and America*
# 1940s & 1950s 9

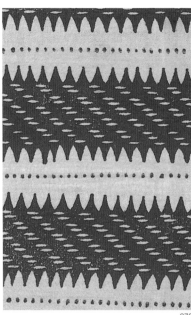

878

880

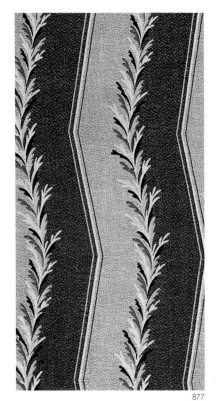

877

879

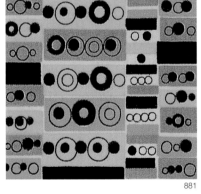

881

**877** *The combination of vertical stripes and plants was very much in vogue during the 1950s. This pattern was used on both textiles and wallpapers, providing a fully coordinated look.*

**878** *Called 'Pointed Pip', this English design is a play on the still-life image of half an apple. Although originally created in the 1930s it was* remarketed in the 1950s, when it became an instant success.

**879** *A detail from a mid-1950s French printed fabric. The broad brush strokes and vibrant colours give it an 'arty' feel.*

**880** *The architect Frank Lloyd Wright designed this screen-printed cotton fabric for F. Schumacher & Co.* in 1957. With its complex play of lines and spaces, it is almost like the ground plan for a Frank Lloyd Wright building.

**881** *Cellular structures are combined with a grid pattern in this detail from a late 1950s fabric, no doubt inspired by contemporary interest in science, technology and architecture.*

**882** *This pattern is essentially a grid – and yet there are no straight lines in sight. It is a clever play on the popular 'architectural' theme, as seen in* **880** *and* **881**. *This American printed cotton was made in the late 1950s.*

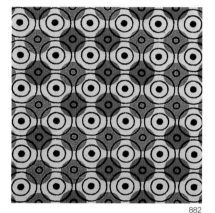
882

884

886

883

885

887

**883** *An array of jungle plants features on this American 1950s fabric. Boldly rendered, the various shapes and strong colours offer the strongest contrast imaginable with the pearl-grey background to the pattern.*

**884** *An American roller-printed cotton fabric made in the late 1950s. 'Oriental'-style patterns such as this,*

*with its debt to Japanese prints, became popular when American servicemen returned from wartime postings in the Far East.*

**885** *A curtain fabric made in France in the early 1950s. Bold floral patterns of this character offered a vivid new option for women who wanted to get rid of their pre-war curtains.*

**886** *Strange shapes reminiscent of kites, balloons and butterflies appear to float in space. The designer of this 1950s pattern was influenced by the art of Joan Miró and Wassily Kandinsky.*

**887** *This printed dress fabric was produced in France in the early 1950s It provided a splash of colour and gaiety after the drab austerity of wartime.*

888

# 1960s & 1970s

**888** *A screen-printed cotton design, called 'Lokki', by the Finnish designer Maija Iola, made in 1961. With its flat, clashing colours, this style came to be known as 'supergraphics'.*

889

**889** *The traditional paisley pattern – an adaptation of a traditional Eastern motif – is printed in acid colours on this 1960s silk. When the Beatles came back from India wearing traditional Indian clothes, complete with paisley-type patterns, designers immediately responded with psychedelic versions such as this.*

**890** *A detail from a late 1960s printed fabric. The design taps into the aesthetics of the Abstract Expressionist painting of the period – lots of loose brushstrokes on a primary-coloured ground.*

890

**891** *The 1960s was not all psychedelia and avant-garde art. This neat little repeat, probably English, evokes the newly fashionable Continental style of home cooking.*

891

These patterns are a reflection of the dramatic social changes and subsequent emphasis on style that exploded into the youth-centred pop culture. The 'Swinging Sixties' drew their inspiration from fashion, the movies, music and art and recycled the images on to textiles and wallpapers. Designs from earlier periods were reworked, scaled up and stylised into the flat, brilliantly coloured patterns so typical of the period. In particular, traditional Indian paisley motifs, Victoriana and Op Art images were transformed into the distinctive patterns we see here. Colour trends developed from the bright psychedelic colours of the early 1960s to the pastels of the 1970s as chemical dyes recreated the muted tones of the natural dyes madder, indigo and weld, producing a palette of peach, pink, pale blue and warm yellow.

*Europe and America*
# 1960s & 1970s 2

**892** *A detail from a printed curtain fabric made in England in the late 1960s. The apple was a popular 1960s motif, used by the Beatles as a logo for their recording company.*

**893** *'Riders', a screen-printed textile designed in 1960 by Marino Marini for Edinburgh Weavers Ltd. Marini was one of the most important Italian sculptors of the post-war period. He was known for his horse-and-rider sculptures, which made reference to Greek and Roman mythology.*

**894** *Broad areas of colour, with soft, uneven edges, are juxtaposed to form an abstract design. This French printed fabric, produced in 1963, pays homage to 'colour field' painters such as Mark Rothko.*

**895** *Reinterpretations of the Art Nouveau style were immensely popular in the 1960s. This screen-printed design on cotton was created in 1969 by Margaret Cannon for Hull Traders Ltd., England.*

**896** *A 1960s French textile design inspired by the popular interest in outer space. Planets, sunspots and solar eclipses appeared on fabrics, ceramics and wallpaper throughout the 1960s and 1970s.*

892

893

895

894

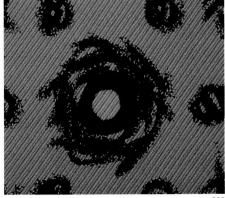

896

897

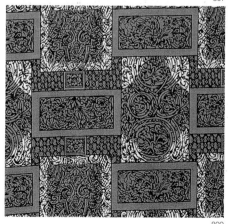

898

899

**897** *The idea of 'dropping out' and living off the land took hold in the 1960s; a young generation of idealists romanticised the joys of smallholdings and self-sufficiency. Traditional in style, this 1960s textile evokes the rural idyll that most would only dream of.*

**898** *A detail from a woven design, 'Crystalline Image', designed in 1962 by the English artist Alan Reynolds. If the starting point was the beauty of crystals and the way they refract light, this idea has been developed to create a highly inventive and complex motif. Similar shapes, albeit in simplified form, were a popular design for light fittings in the 1960s.*

**899** *If you look closely at this 1960s textile design you can see all sorts of Celtic-inspired motifs in the background pattern. The hippie generation saw essential links between 'living the real life', self-sufficiency, folk music and Celtic art. Dragons, the Green Man, runic signs and references to myths and magic all started to make an appearance in patterns at this time.*

*Europe and America*
# 1960s & 1970s 3

901

902

903

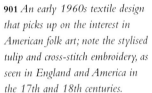

904

**900** *'Avon', a textile design from 1960 by Cecil Collins; the reference is to Stratford-upon-Avon, the home of William Shakespeare. The figures are Shakespearean characters: exciting new stagings ensured Shakespeare a new role in interior design.*

**901** *An early 1960s textile design that picks up on the interest in American folk art; note the stylised tulip and cross-stitch embroidery, as seen in England and America in the 17th and 18th centuries.*

**902** *Watery colours and forms float across the surface of this 1960s printed textile, inspired by the work of Wassily Kandinsky. Few people had heard of the abstract artist until his work was brought out in poster form, and patterns in the Kandinsky style began to emerge.*

**903** *With its patches of colour and sketchy pattern this 1960s design has a 'homemade' quality to it,*

900

although it is commercially printed. It was produced to reflect the popular interest in dyeing your own fabrics.

**904** A silk-screen printed textile design by Victor Vasarely made in 1962. Vasarely was a leading Op Art painter. Artists of the 1960s Op Art movement created abstract paintings that explored optical effects, resulting in strong illusions of movement and three-dimensional form.

**905** A detail from a printed paisley design, made in England in the late 1960s. Paisley was considered to be old-fashioned – only to be seen on grandmother's shawls and dad's cravat – until the Beatles started wearing it, and then suddenly it was back in fashion. The manufacturers updated it by printing it in brilliant colours.

**906** 'Prince of Quince Terence', a screen-printed textile designed in 1965 by Juliet Glyn-Smith

for Conran Fabrics. The company produced patterns that were designed to appeal to the young bohemian set.

**907** This design, sometimes referred to as 'feathers', is instantly datable to the late 1960s, yet very little is known of its origins. It was used in a huge range of applications: on furnishings, dress fabrics and printed plastics. This detail is from a textile sample that was made in the 1970s.

906

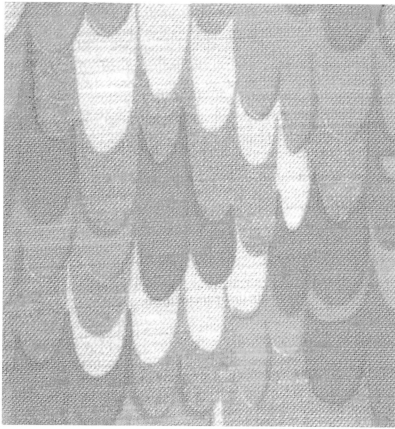

907

905

*Europe and America*
# 1960s &
# 1970s 4

**908** *A 1960s English printed textile that draws its inspiration from designs on English medieval encaustic tiles and Victorian 'medieval' tiles – the sort of tiles seen in English cathedrals and Victorian villas. During the 1960s there was a revival of interest in Victoriana.*

**909** *The traditional paisley design has been reinterpreted in this 1960s textile. Compare it with* **910** *and see how it has been quieted with softer shapes and muted colours to suit a broader market.*

**910** *While the starting point for this printed textile is traditional Indian and English Victorian paisley, the designer updated it to suit the swinging pop generation of the 1960s – lots of bright psychedelic colours and overblown motifs.*

**911** *'Macrogauze 26', a woven wall hanging made by Peter Collingwood in 1968. Look carefully at the pattern and you will be able to see how the design plays tricks with the eye: the darker diamond pattern appears to float above the lighter one.*

**912** *'Simple Solar', a textile design by Shirley Craven from 1968. The design is influenced by the stylised 'cloud' imagery seen in the Beatles film* Yellow Submarine.

**913** *A detail from a 1960s paisley print. While many of the traditional Indian motifs, such as the teardrop-shape* boteh, *are still present, the design has been simplified and rendered in typical 'flower power' colours: shades of orange on a dark brown background.*

**914** *Bold sweeps of colour form the pattern on this printed fabric, made in France in the late 1960s. It reflects the revival of interest in hand-painted textiles at that time.*

908

910

912

909

911

913

*Europe and America*
# 1960s &
# 1970s 5

**915** *This painterly, impressionistic pattern was influenced by abstract artists such as Emilio Vedova and the early Jackson Pollock. The detail comes from a printed French textile made in the early 1970s. This textile was aimed at young consumers.*

**916** *A detail from a French print made in the early 1970s. The design springs from the contemporary interest in hallucinogenic drugs such as LSD; users would experience mind-altering visions. In his widely read book* Heaven and Hell, *Aldous Huxley described a vision of 'fire-bright ribbons of colour' experienced under the influence of LSD.*

**917** *You can just about make out the paisley motif – the* boteh *– in this Italian printed textile from 1966. The design has been brightly coloured, however, and blown up to huge proportions. The effect is like an explosion of colour – tailored to the taste of the time.*

**918** *The flower was the primary symbol of the 1960s. Young people wore flowers in their hair, sewed flower patches on to their jeans, and poked flowers into the muzzles of guns to protest against the Vietnam War. Childlike drawings of huge flowers were popular; this design was made in France in 1964.*

915

916

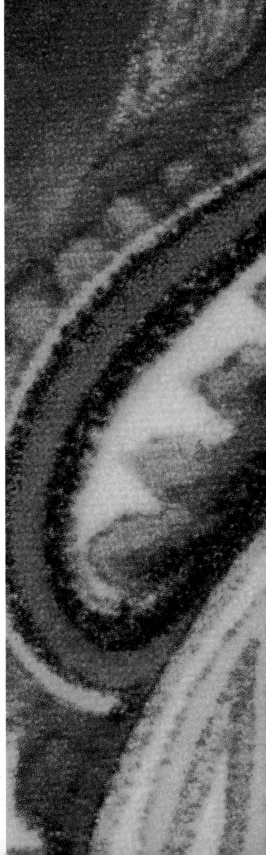

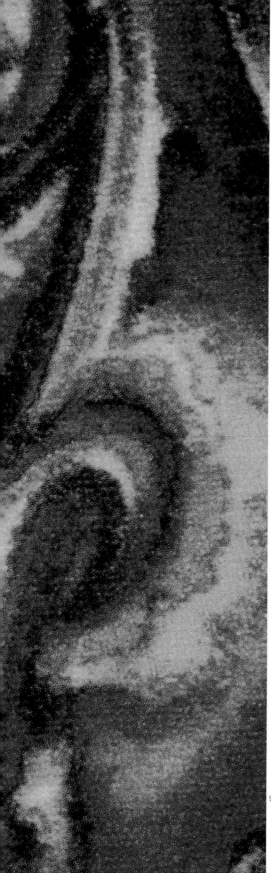

**919** *A detail from a French fabric, dated about 1965. The design springs from the popular interest in Expressionism and Impressionism – especially in the work of Van Gogh – in the way that colour and line have been used to express movement. The motifs used in this design appear to shimmer and dance.*

**920** *A design for a textile, gouache on paper, made in the United States in the 1960s. The swirling psychedelic shapes and bands of fluorescent colour are associated with hallucinogenic drugs. Gradually designs of this character came to be used in and on everything from textiles and adhesive decals to comics and sweet wrappers.*

**921** *Flower patterns could be cool and sophisticated as well as simple and childlike. This 1970s textile design draws its inspiration from a mix of psychedelic graphics and the motifs seen in traditional Japanese art.*

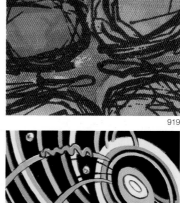

919

920

918

921

917

*Europe and America*

# 1960s & 1970s 6

**922** *Simple folk-art patterns enjoyed a surge of popularity in the 1970s, and are clearly one of the influences for this floral design. The naive flower shapes with clean outlines seem to represent simplicity and innocence. Patterns of this sort were well-matched to the little-girl-lost look of the female models of the period. This fabric was designed in the 1970s.*

**923** *A detail of a French printed textile from 1963. Like many designs of the period it is based on the paisley motif, loosely rendered in a range of ochres and rich browns.*

**924** *A 1960s American psychedelic design, gouache on paper, that taps into, or perhaps was inspired by,*

the drug culture. Acid users describe seeing 'shattered colours…like multicoloured images seen in a broken mirror.'

**925** *Flowers – especially simply drawn, colourful ones – are the quintessential symbol of the 1960s. Artists painted them; pop stars sang about them; cars, kitchens and cushions were all decorated with them. This detail comes from a fabric made in the late 1960s.*

**926** *A detail from a screen-printed textile, called 'Cavallo', designed in 1960 by Marino Marini for Edinburgh Weavers Ltd. The motif is a sketchy version of one of Marini's favourite themes: horse and rider. The highly stylised*

922     923     925     927

924     926     928

drawing, with the elements reduced to their bare essentials, resembles prehistoric cave painting, another strong interest of Marini's.

**927–928** *Two screen-printed textile designs, made in England in the very late 1950s/early 1960s. Both designs exploit the recently introduced printing technology that enabled designers to turn photographic images into screen prints. A designer could take a photograph and print it on just about anything, from biscuit tins to decals. While the technique soon fell from favour in terms of textiles – apart from T-shirts and some dress fabrics – it was taken up in a big way by the growing packaging industry.*

**929** *Traditional block-printing inspired this mid-1960s printed textile: the solid black motifs look as though they have been stamped on to the fabric. The motifs themselves derive from the photographic technique of pulling images out of focus so as to distort them. The resultant shape is mysterious – very much like a psychiatrist's ink-blot, whereby one person sees the images as old encaustic tiles, while another sees them as calligraphy, aerial photographs, and so on. The result is an intriguing and visually dynamic design.*

929

*Europe and America*
# 1960s & 1970s 7

**930** *This 1970s French fabric is a copy of a traditional chintz design.* Chinz, *a glazed cotton cloth usually patterned with flowers, fruits or birds, was imported from India in the 17th century and subsequently produced in England. While young couples in the 1950s had rejected chintz as too dated for their own use, in the 1960s and 1970s there was a strong revival of interest in all things chintzy, floral and Victorian for both clothing and the home.*

**931** *A detail from a printed textile made in France in the 1960s. This design draws its inspiration from the interest in hand-painted textiles.*

930

931

**932** *A detail from a printed textile, a prize-winning design called 'Inglewood' by Humphrey Spender, produced in the early 1960s. The design picks up on the growing interest in self-sufficiency and going back to the land.*

**933** *The densely packed blooms and teardrop-shaped petals on this design are loosely based on patterns seen on Afghan carpets and Turkish wall tiles. In the 1960s people were beginning to travel to exotic places and were becoming interested in ethnic designs and motifs. This roller-printed cotton fabric was made in England in the early 1960s.*

**934** *Another design inspired by exotic travel and ethnic crafts. Compared with pattern* **933***, however, this pattern sticks much more closely to the original. The motifs are similar to those seen in Turkish and Afghan rugs. This detail comes from a French roller-printed rayon fabric made in the late 1960s. Young people at this time liked to decorate their rooms and flats with 'primitive' objects and designs – drums, masks, carvings and of course fabrics that showed tribal motifs.*

**935** *An English fabric from an early 1960s sample book showing materials suitable for men's pajamas, dressing gowns and scarves. The pattern is the ever-popular paisley, an adaptation of the traditional Eastern* boteh *motif. Unlike later psychedelic versions of the paisley design (see, for example,* **905** *on page 291 and* **910** *on page 292), this version is traditional in colouring.*

**936** *The ongoing fashion for wearing camouflage as street clothing had its beginnings in the late 1950s and early 1960s, when students purchased many of their clothes from army surplus stores. This detail comes from a Swiss army uniform camouflage fabric made in the 1960s.*

936

932

934

933

935

*Europe and America*
# 1960s & 1970s 8

**937** In the 1960s, art schools were especially conscious of newly available, and very vivid, permanent chemical dyes. Many contemporary designers used the sharp, new colours available, sometimes grouping them together to dazzling effect. This is an early 1960s printed dress fabric, probably English.

**938** A detail from an American camouflage worn by soldiers in the 1960s. Some American students wore camouflage ironically, as both an anti-war protest and a way of provoking comment.

**939** A traditional floral design is given a brightly coloured makeover. While 1960s art schools wanted to throw out the old, many traditional printing companies simply adapted existing designs. This detail is from an early 1960s printed fabric.

**940** A 1970s American printed textile that draws its inspiration from artists like Victor Vasarely, who used squares, circles, diamonds and ellipses to create a harmonious overall composition.

**941** This design has its roots in the work of European and American

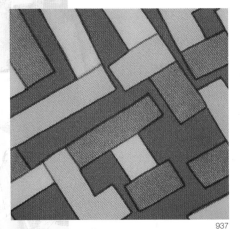

937

940

938

941

939

942

943

944

945

craft potters who were making and using stamps to create impressed designs. Potters such as Bernard Leach were inspired by the signature stamps found in traditional Japanese raku pottery. This fabric was made in France in the late 1960s.

**942** Intense hues of orange and red lend an almost luminous quality to this late 1960s English fabric. It is inspired in part by the work of French artist Auguste Herbin, who combined geometric abstraction with a love of optical effects.

**943** 'Stones of Bath', a 1960s printed design by the English artist John Piper. He cited his starting point as the city of Bath in England, 'the character of the buildings, and the drama and mystery of city life.'

**944** The rhythm and repetition seen in the work of Pop artists such as Andy Warhol was sometimes echoed in commercial patterns, such as this one from the late 1960s.

**945** A fabric from an early 1970s sample book, probably English. The flower motifs and psychedelic colours of the 1960s were used well into the following decade.

*Europe and America*
# 1960s &
# 1970s 9

947

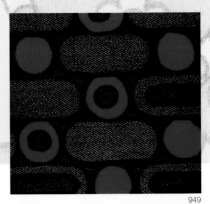

949

946

948

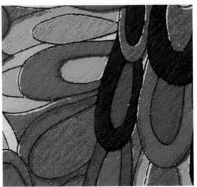

950

951

**946, 948** *These 1970s prints are both psychedelic variations on the paisley pattern, a reworking of the Indian boteh motif. The design on the left,* **946,** *blows up the boteh to huge proportions in order to incorporate that hippie favourite, the 'lazy-daisy'.*

**947** *This French cotton print has the hand-drawn, almost homemade look*

*that was very popular in the mid-1960s. Folk arts and traditional crafts enjoyed a revival at this time.*

**949** *The round-edged shapes in this printed fabric have a parallel in the rounded, plastic forms that began to emerge in the 1960s, as seen on toys, tableware and the like. This print was made in France about 1965.*

**950** *In some ways an ultra-stylised paisley, this late 1960s pattern can also be seen as a variant of the 'feather' motif seen in* **907** *on page 291.*

**951** *By the late 1970s the fashion for hot psychedelic colours had largely given way to a softer, more neutral palette, though many of the outline patterns, like this one, remained unchanged.*

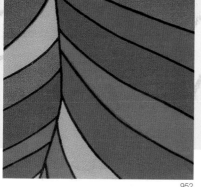

952

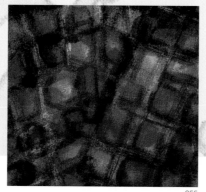

955

953

954

956

957

**952** *The new chemical dyes of the 1960s made possible all sorts of vibrant colour combinations. This Italian printed silk fabric dates from 1965.*

**953** *This colourful screen-printed floral textile has the somewhat incongruous title 'Jupiter'. It was made in 1966 by Isabel M. Colquhoun for Simpson and Godlee Ltd., England.*

**954** *A psychedelic paisley made in the late 1960s. Indian-inspired pattern and acid colours were used on everything from wallpaper to headscarves.*

**955** *The blurred quality of this 1961 design recalls the psychedelic 'coloured liquid' effects used in 1960s movies. It can also be seen in that quintessential 1960s item, the lava lamp.*

**956** *The butterfly was a classic 1970s motif, used in literally dozens of applications. This French fabric features machine-embroidered butterflies on a woven denim ground.*

**957** *'Lunar Rocket', a 1969 design by Eddie Squires. The U.S. lunar landing that year was a huge source of inspiration for artists and designers.*

*Europe and America*
# 1960s &
# 1970s 10

**958** *Dabs of luminous colour create a shimmering effect on this mid-1970s printed fabric. The design taps into the interest in the art of the Impressionists, the French innovators of the late 19th century, who used short brush strokes to capture fleeting light effects.*

**959** *An interest in art school culture and watercolour painting inspired this 1970s design. If you weren't an art student and couldn't paint, then at least you could wear clothes and furnish your house in a style that suggested an artistic sense.*

**960** *At first glance this 1960s design looks like a standard paisley pattern. Look carefully, however, and you will find daisies – the decade's quintessential motif – within the teardrop boteh shapes.*

**961** *A Hawaiian shirt fabric made in the early 1970s and designed for casual wear. The decade was the first to offer really affordable air travel and exotic holidays. This design is intended to convey the impression that its wearer is a paid-up member of the jet set.*

**962** *Detail from a fabric made in France in the late 1960s. The painterly design combines bold, swiftly drawn lines with vibrant colours. Apples were a popular 1960s and 1970s motif.*

**963** *A detail from a printed textile entitled 'Petrus', made in 1967 by Peter Hall for Heals, England. The inspiration for the design is the mythical source of all knowledge – a holy spring that bubbled up like a many-tiered fountain.*

**964** *Out-of-focus patterns were popular in the 1960s and 1970s, and similar imagery was used in the decades' art movies. This sort of pattern, seen out of the corner of your eye, looks definitely representational.*

958

960

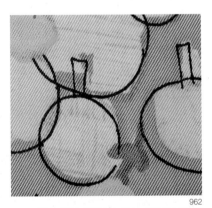

962

959

961

963

964

*Europe and America*

# 1960s &
# 1970s 11

965

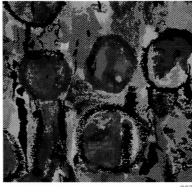

967

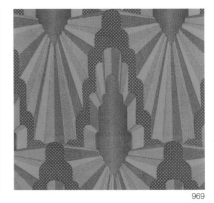

969

966

968

970

**965** *A printed silk 'brush-stroke' design, made in France in the late 1960s. Designs of this type had their roots in the new printing technologies and dyes, and in the popular fashion for richly coloured art silks.*

**966** *A detail from a wall hanging, made in America in 1961 by the renowned textile designer Jack Lenor*

*Larson. The pattern has its roots in traditional Scandinavian folk art – woven tapestries. The motifs, with their mix of enclosed space and sharp points, look as if they also have links to Northwest Coast Native American art.*

**967–968** *Two French 'modern art' fabrics made in the mid-1960s. Both reflect the fashion for abstract, painterly*

*designs and for blurry, out-of-focus effects. The design above (**967**), in particular, looks as though it has been made with ink-blots.*

**969** *'Archway', a fabric that was designed in 1968 by Eddie Squires for Warner & Sons, England. This fabric design taps into a whole range of references, including psychedelia,*

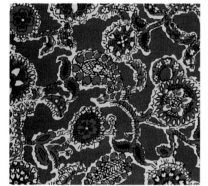

971

973

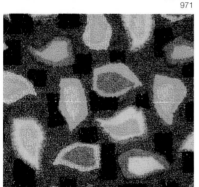

972

974

*Art Deco and poster design – especially the work of the Japanese artist Hirokatsu Hijikata.*

**970** *Although partly abstract, this 1960s fabric design conjures up images of the Mediterranean in its Dufy-esque details. The introduction of low-cost flights to destinations such as Spain and Greece meant that ordinary people*

*began to get a taste of the southern European lifestyle. And when they returned home they were enthusiastic about fabrics that reminded them of their holidays.*

**971** *This late 1960s English fabric is derived from a traditional paisley design. However, if you look closely you will see that at the centre of each*

*conventional teardrop motif, the pattern detail is made up from minute hearts and flowers. Patterns of this character, printed on to light poplins and lawns, were used for summer dresses.*

**972** *Yet another pattern – this one on a 1970s dress fabric – which recalls a traditional paisley. In this case, though, the motifs look as though they have been made from scraps of torn paper – a popular art technique at the time – making up a kind of paisley-style collage. The luminous colours give the motifs a flame-like quality.*

**973** *A detail from a printed fabric of the mid-1970s. The pattern seems, at first glance, to recall one of the jungle prints so popular in the 1950s, but in a very much abstracted form. Note the rose-like motif bottom left.*

**974** *Drawn lines – like the scribbles of an architect – and blobs of neutral colour with apparently random splotches of pink are combined to create a dynamic pattern on this 1960s English dress fabric. The designer may have been inspired by artists such as Mairia Elena Vieira da Silva and Fritz Winter, who produced similar works from the 1950s onwards. This abstract mix of graphic line and colour was a popular formula in the 1960s and can be found on furnishing fabrics as well as on clothing.*

*Europe and America*

# 1960s & 1970s 12

**975–976** *Two fabrics made in the mid-1960s, probably from France or Italy. These designs were produced when Continental art fabrics were particularly modish. Fashion-conscious women no longer wanted recognisable motifs – they were more interested in bold, abstract designs that made a statement about their wearers.*

**977** *Black and white shapes play tricks with the eye in this 1969 fabric by Margaret Cannon. It takes its cue from the Op Art movement.*

**978** *This screen-printed fabric from the 1970s relates to traditional Japanese stencil-printed fabrics. Note the characteristic Japanese*

979

975

977

976

978

980

981

983

982

984

counterchange effect, with the fish motifs featured both in white on black and black on white.

**979** In this 1960s fabric, sketchy lines combine with bold patches of colour to create a bohemian feel. A popular style at the time: compare with **962**, page 304.

**980** While this late 1960s printed fabric is a reworking of a traditional woven check, it also taps into the contemporary 'grid' aesthetic of modern steel-and-glass architecture.

**981** A 1960s fabric design with an odd but very characteristic pattern consisting of a mix of images and type, the former overlaying the latter. This particular trend lasted into the 1970s, but was obsolete by the end of the decade.

**982** A detail from an English printed textile made in the late 1960s. This design harks back to the late 1940s, when fashions were more reserved and colours were muted. The colour palette, in particular, is unusual for the decade.

**983** Blocks of colour are used to create a three-dimensional illusion in this 1970s woven textile. The design relates to contemporary interest in geometrical forms, used with particular emphasis in the field of graphic design.

**984** A characteristic 1970s reworking of the classic English paisley. In this design, the centre of each boteh motif explodes into an extravagantly coloured iris, itself made up of several motifs joined in a style reminiscent of Art Nouveau flowers. The combination of references gives special energy to this pattern.

985

**985** *'Cote d'Azur', a 1983 design by Collier Campbell. The French Riviera is evoked by the colourful pattern of palms, awnings, and glimpses of blue sky and sea.*

**986** *A traditional palette of indigo, red, and white was used for this 1990 Collier Campbell design, 'Gypsy Dance'. The roses and patchwork tablecloths pay homage to folk art.*

**987** *This Collier Campbell design, 'Zuni', was sold between 1987 and 2000. The grey, taupe, and brown shapes, with their irregular outlines, create a subtle design that perfectly captures the woven pattern that inspired it.*

**988** *This frenetic pattern from 1982, entitled 'Gabon', was designed by Natalie du Pasquier for Memphis, the influential Italian design collective. She described her design as 'a jerky dance' taking inspiration from rock music, comics and African textiles.*

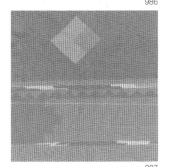

986

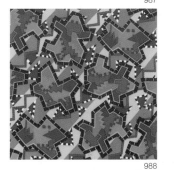

987

988

*Europe and America*
# 1980s to the Present

This period has seen a steady revival in the decorative arts to offer designers artistic and commercial success in the burgeoning interiors and clothing markets. Throughout the 1980s artists and designers were revisiting every historical archive at their disposal for document designs that helped them to remodel the past and create an all-pervasive 'country house style'. A reaction to chintz came with the 1990s minimalist movement, which concentrated almost exclusively on texture and tone. This trend has reversed since the start of the new millennium as designers revisit patterns from around the world, using a vast colour palette and reflecting the shared levels of reference in today's global community. Increasingly, computers have been used to manipulate designs, allowing instant changes to colour, scale and layout.

*Europe and America*
# 1980s to the Present

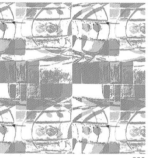
989

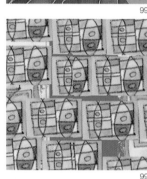
993

990

994

**989** Bernice Christoph designed this screen-printed furnishing fabric, 'Tabasco', in 1987. Its lively design elements suggest torn paper streamers.

**990** With its blurred abstract shapes and muted colouring, this pattern by Dru Cole is rather reminiscent of 1950s designs. It was manipulated on a computer and printed digitally.

**991** 'Blackbird', a bold, naturalistic design by Collier Campbell. Printed on to silk as a furnishing fabric, it was launched in 2002.

**992** The digital age was the obvious inspiration for this furnishing fabric, designed by Leo Santos-Shaw and Margrét Adolfsdottir in 1999.

**993** This 2000 design by Dru Cole was printed using a wide-body digital printer. The images of oak leaves were hand-painted on to silk and subsequently manipulated by computer.

**994** Dru Cole designed this pattern in 2002. The computer-manipulated design features multicoloured abstract shapes in an irregular repeat.

**995** A section of a dragonfly's wing, enlarged and manipulated by computer, formed the basis for this design. It was created by the Finnish designer Stefan Lindfors in 1997.

**996** Sun-like orbs are placed next to a roughly drawn indigo stripe in this bold 1992 design by Lena Bergstrom.

**997–1000** These four patterns were all created in 2002 by Chadissa Greenaway, using digital techniques. They form part of a collection of abstract designs for interiors. Pattern **998** was initially based on cut paper shapes, which were subsequently manipulated on a computer. Pattern **1000** demonstrates the intricate results that can be achieved using computer-aided design; the cell-like structures, echoing organic and architectural shapes, are sensitively coloured to produce an intricate pattern.

991

995

992

996

997

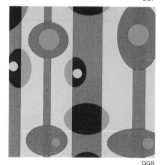

998

999

1000

# Glossary

**ABSTRACT EXPRESSIONISM** An American art movement of the 1940s and 1950s, in which the artists' expression of their feelings informed their abstract creations.

**ACANTHUS** A stylised representation of an acanthus leaf, often used in scroll form.

**APPLIQUÉ** A decorative technique for applying, or laying on, shaped pieces of fabric to a ground material to create a design, usually by stitching.

**ARABESQUE** A motif of intricately intertwined vines, tendrils, or branches.

**ART DECO** A style of decorative art typical of the 1920s and 1930s, characterised by sleek forms, geometric patterns, and simplified lines; the name was derived from the 1925 International Exhibition in Paris that showed 'des Arts Décoratifs'.

**ART NOUVEAU** A decorative form of 'new art' that was prevalent from about 1890 to 1910, and which combined curvilinear plant forms and asymmetrical lines; a tendril with 'whiplash' lines emanating from it was a recurrent motif.

**ARTS AND CRAFTS** A British art movement, inspired by William Morris, that sought a return to the ideals of medieval craftmanship, with designs drawing heavily on the natural world; the name was derived from the Arts and Crafts Exhibition Society founded in 1888 to promote the decorative arts.

**BACKSTRAP LOOM** An ancient weaving device used to create intricate weaving patterns; its name is derived from the belt or strap support that fits around the back of the weaver, who controls the tension of the warp with his or her body.

**BARKCLOTH** A thin, papery cloth with a dense, textured weave, made from the inner bark of specific trees; also known as *tapa*. Designs are first carved in wood, then transferred to the barkcloth by rubbing the dye through to it.

**BAROQUE** The exuberant style of decoration that was prevalent in Europe during the 17th and early 18th centuries.

**BAST** A linen-like plant fibre derived from the inner bark, husks, and other parts of plants such as hemp and jute.

**BATIK** An Indonesian method of producing designs on cloth by applying a wax or starch resist to the fabric before it is dyed, so that only those parts that are unprotected receive the dye in each successive dipping.

**BAUHAUS** A German school of art and architecture, dating from 1919 to 1933, which aimed to integrate art and technology in design.

**BLOCK PRINTING** An ancient and time-consuming method of hand printing, whereby patterns are cut in relief in wooden blocks, after which the colour is transferred to the cloth by hitting the block with a mallet; such cloth is known as *yukata* in Japan.

**BOTEH** A teardrop or cone motif widely used in India and Asia as a symbol of fertility and creativity; also known as a *buta*. In the West it is described as a 'paisley' design.

**BROCADE** A heavy silk fabric with the appearance of a raised design.

*BUTA see* **BOTEH**

**BYZANTINE** Relating to the art and architecture of the eastern Roman Empire, from c. 33 CE up to 1453.

**CALICO** A cotton cloth, originally imported from Calicut in southern India.

*CANTING* **WORK** A technique in which liquid wax, heated in a kettle-like *canting*, is trailed over fabric to mark out the design. The fabric is then dipped in dye (the dye not penetrating the wax trail), then ironed to remove the wax.

**CARTOUCHE** A decorative frame with scroll-like ornament.

**CELTIC KNOT** *see* **EVERLASTING KNOT**

**CHI (QI)** An Eastern concept representing the life force or energy of all animate things.

**CHINOISERIE** A European style of decoration based on Chinese design; it was very popular in Europe in the 18th and 19th centuries.

**CHINTZ** A glazed cotton, which may be solid in colour, printed with flowers or stripes or embossed.

**CLASSICAL** Referring to artistic styles with their origins in ancient Greece or Rome, or inspired by them.

**CLOISONNÉ** A technique for decorating with enamel, which is inlaid in metal-framed compartments on to a copper base; after firing, the colours melt to form brilliant ponds of colour.

**COLLAGE** A design created from assembled fragments (often paper) applied to a flat surface to create a three-dimensional effect.

**COLOURWAY** One of a range of colours in which a fabric is available.

**CONSTRUCTIVISM** A Russian abstract art movement founded in about 1913 by Vladimir Tatlin, advocating industrial materials, machine production, and abstract forms.

**COUCHING** A style of embroidery where thread is laid on the surface of the fabric and secured by stitches forming a pattern.

**'COUNTERCHANGE' DESIGN** One in which a certain colour of motif and ground are reversed in another part of the design to balance the elements (for example, by using black on white, and white on black, motifs).

**CRETONNE** A colourfully printed heavy cotton or linen fabric primarily used for curtains or slipcovers.

**CREWELWORK** Embroidery done with crewel wool, a fine worsted yarn, on a cotton or linen ground.

**CUBISM** An early 20th-century art movement, originated by Picasso and Braque, in which three-dimensional images were built up on the canvas using fragmented solids and volumes.

**DAMASK** A patterned woven fabric with a design that is visible on both sides; it was originally introduced from China to Europe via Damascus, hence its name.

**DECORATIVE ARTS** A collective term for ornamental art forms such as ceramics, enamels, glass, furniture, jewellery, metalwork, and textiles, especially when used for interior decoration.

**DIAPER** An allover ornamental pattern, made up of repeated geometric shapes.

**DOUBLE-CLOTH** Reversible fabric created by interweaving two layers of cloth at the same time on the same loom.

**DRY PAINTING** A technique for creating designs using coloured sand; such designs were often made by Native American shamans for use in their religious ceremonies, featuring zigzag and cross motifs; also known as sand painting.

**EGG-AND-TONGUE** A decorative design in which egg-shaped and tongue-shaped forms alternate.

**EVERLASTING KNOT** A motif comprising complex interlaced ribboned forms that lead seamlessly into one another; also known as the Celtic or magic knot.

**EXPRESSIONISM** An art form that turned away from expressing external reality and towards expressing the artist's emotions and reactions.

**FOLIATED** Decorated with, or shaped like, leaf ornaments or foils.

**FOULARD** A lightweight fabric traditionally printed with a repeating small-scale pattern.

**FRETTING** A cut-out technique used to create a tracery effect, which was popular at the start of the 20th century.

**FUTURISM** An Italian art movement founded in 1909, which glorified machinery, science and speed.

**GERMANTOWN** A commercially produced yarn made in Germantown, Philadelphia, that was used in weaving Navajo blankets.

**GOTHIC** A European style of decoration, which lasted from the mid-12th to the 15th century, characterised by pointed forms and foliate motifs.

**GOTHIC REVIVAL** A revival of the medieval Gothic style of decoration, which lasted from the mid-18th to the mid-19th century.

**GOUACHE** A heavy, opaque watercolour paint that creates a matt surface.

**GREEK KEY** A running fretwork pattern; also known as the running dog by Turkoman rug weavers.

**GROTESQUE** An extravagant ornament incorporating putti, animals, cornucopiae, flowing tendrils, swags, scrolls, and mythical figures in fantastic forms.

**GROUND** The surface of a textile on to which motifs or other materials (such as embroidery) are applied.

*GUL* An octagonal lozenge motif widely used in Persia.

**HAND-WOVEN** Fabric that is created on a manually operated loom.

# Glossary

**HEMP** A coarse-fibred cloth made from the *Cannabis sativa* plant.

**HERATI** A stylised rosette, often used as a motif on carpets in the Caspian region.

**IKAT** An Indonesian method of creating designs by binding the resist material (to the warp and/or the weft) at intervals around the yarn prior to dyeing, to produce a geometric pattern; such cloth is known as *kasuri* in Japan.

**IMPRESSIONISM** A French art movement of the late 19th century, which aimed to create a true rendition of what the artist actually saw, often through the direct study of nature and light effects.

**INLAY** A thin piece of material embedded in a depressed ground.

**INTARSIA** A form of decorative inlay work using wood and ivory, developed in Italy in the 15th century.

**KASURI** *see* Ikat

**LINO PRINTING** A technique in which a design is cut in linoleum before being printed.

**LITHOGRAPH** A print from a stone or metal plate, using a technique that depends on the resistance of oil to water.

**MAGIC KNOT** *see* **EVERLASTING KNOT**

**MAYAN** Relating to a native civilisation of southern Mexico and Central America, which flourished from the 3rd to the 9th centuries CE.

**MEDIEVAL** Relating to the Middle Ages, the period that occurred in Europe between the disintegration of the Roman Empire in the 5th century and the Renaissance in the 15th century.

**MOTIF** A dominant or recurring shape that is repeated in a pattern.

**OP ART** An abstract American art movement of the 1960s, which created the illusion of movement in a painting through the use of precise geometrical forms and optical phenomena.

**ORGANIC** Inspired by, or based on, natural forms.

**OVOLO** A molding with the rounded part comprising a quarter of a circle.

**PAISLEY** The traditional Asian *boteh* or teardop pattern, which was originally used in India to decorate painted and printed fabric and woven cashmere shawls; during the 19th century imitations of the Kashmir shawls were woven at Paisley in Scotland.

**PASTORAL** Relating to the rural life, often in an idealised or conventionalised way.

**PILE** A looped yarn (cut or uncut) on the surface of a fabric.

**POP ART** A British and American art movement from the late 1950s to early 1970s, which took its inspiration from popular culture and consumerist images of modern urbanised life.

**PRE-COLUMBIAN** Relating to the native civilisations that existed in Mexico, Central America and the Andean area of South America prior to European colonisation in the 16th century.

**'PRIMITIVE' ART** Art that is simple, naive or unsophisticated in style and approach; often influenced by folk or tribal art.

**PUTTO** (**PLURAL:** *PUTTI*) A plump, naked young boy or cherub, often winged; *putti* were a popular feature of Renaissance and Baroque art.

**QUATREFOIL** A four-petalled flower or a leaf comprising four leaflets.

**RAFFIA** The stripped leaves of the Raphia palm.

**RAYON** An inexpensive artificial fibre produced from cellulose.

**RENAISSANCE** The period of European history that lasted from the mid-15th century to the end of the 16th century, and which signified the revival of interest (literally, the 'rebirth') in arts and letters.

**REPEAT** A complete unit of a pattern in a repeating design.

**RESIST** A protective coating (such as wax, paste or starch) applied to fabric in order to prevent certain areas from accepting dye.

**ROCOCO** The playful style of decoration that developed in France in the early 18th century, characterised by swirls, scrolls, arabesques and shells.

**ROLLER PRINTING** A technique in which a design is applied to fabric by engraved copper rollers as it passes around a metal cylinder.

**ROMANESQUE** A European style of decoration lasting from the 9th to the 12th century, typified by round forms and linear stylizations.

**ROUNDEL** A circular device.

**RUNNING DOG** *see* **GREEK KEY**

**SAND PAINTING** *see* **DRY PAINTING**

**SATEEN** A glossy fabric resembling satin, in which a smooth surface is created by floating weft yarns over multiple ends.

**SCREEN PRINTING** A form of stencilling, in which a fine mesh is stretched over a frame with stencils on the underside of the frame; the colour is then forced through the mesh in those areas of the screen not blocked out by the stencil.

**SCROLL** A ribbon-like motif in the shape of a partly rolled scroll of paper.

**SELVEDGE** The long, finished edge of a fabric, which is unlikely to fray and runs parallel to the warp.

**SHIBORU** *see* **TIE-DYEING**

**SGRAFFITO** Decorative work created by removing parts of the outer layers of material to reveal different underlying colours.

**SLIT TAPESTRY** A technique in which a pattern is created by running weft threads across the width of the warp, with slits where an individual weft thread loops around a warp thread to make its return journey.

**STENCIL PRINTING** A technique in which colour is applied to material through the open area of a cut-out motif that is laid over the surface to be printed.

**STRAPWORK** A form of ornamentation consisting of interlaced bands.

**STRIP-CLOTH** Long, narrow lengths of fabric woven on small looms; they are joined edge to edge, often in complex arrangements, to create square or rectangular covers.

**SWASTIKA** An equal-armed cross, with the arms bent at right angles, which stemmed from the Pacific region, but has been widely used throughout the world as a symbol of good luck and well being; also known as the wind vane or vane-swastika.

**TAPA** *see* **BARKCLOTH**

**TARTAN** A cloth (usually woollen) with symmetrical patterns that historically represented different Scottish clans.

**TESSELLATED** Formed of square pieces like an ornamental mosaic.

**TIE-DYEING** A technique for hand-dyeing textiles by sewing and binding areas of the fabric so that they resist the dye; known as *shiboru* in Japan.

**'TURNOVER' PATTERN** A pattern in which a motif is flipped, either horizontally or vertically.

**UKIYO-E** A style of Japanese printing and painting that depicted scenes from everyday life and was popular between the 17th and 19th centuries.

**VANE-SWASTIKA** *see* **SWASTIKA**

**VELVETEEN** A close-cut fabric similar to velvet, although in velveteen it is the looped weft threads that are cut to create the pile, whereas in velvet it is the warp threads.

**VICTORIANA** Bric-à-brac and other possessions typical of the Victorian age; Victoriana underwent a revival of interest in the 1960s.

**WARP** Yarns that run the length of a piece of cloth.

**WARP-FACED** Fabric in which the warp predominates on one or both sides.

**WEFT** Yarns that run horizontally across a piece of cloth; they interlace at right angles with the warp.

**WEFT-FACED** Fabric in which the weft predominates on one or both sides.

**WILLOW PATTERN** A blue design of Chinese character, but English origin; it was widely used on china from the late 18th century.

**WIND VANE** *see* **SWASTIKA**

**WOODBLOCK** A design cut in relief on wood, so that ink may be transferred from the raised surface to the material.

**YIN-YANG SYMBOL** A symbol representing the two complementary forces in the universe, according to Chinese Taoism: dark and light, passive and active, male and female.

**YUKATA** *see* **BLOCK PRINTING**

**ZIL-I-SOLTAN** A vase of flowers motif, widely used in Indian and Persian designs and associated in the latter country with royalty.

# Index

# Acknowledgements

The Publishers are grateful to the many individuals who have lent material from their collections for the illustrations and also wish to thank:

Dru Cole for access to her collection and the original artwork of her designs on page 312.

Collier Campbell for their designs on pages 310-12.

Chadissa Greenaway for the original artwork of her designs on page 313.

Hogback Trading Post: page 141 (top right).

Hubbell Trading Post: pages 144 (bottom), 145 (top left and right).

The Montreal Museum of Fine Arts/Liliane and David M. Stewart Collection (D86.166.1): page 311 (bottom).

Die Neue Sammlung, The Museum of Design, Munich: page 312 (top left).

Ohio University/Private collection on permanent loan: pages 141 (bottom left and bottom right).

Private collection: pages 140–1.

Santos & Adolfsdottir: page 312 (bottom left).

The Southern Museum, Los Angeles, California: pages 140, 141(top left),142, 143, 145 (bottom left and bottom right).

Tekstilmuseet: The Swedish Museum of Textile History, Boras: page 312 (bottom right).